Stronger

Stronger

Adapting America's China Strategy in an Age of Competitive Interdependence

Ryan Hass

Yale UNIVERSITY PRESS

New Haven & London

Published with assistance from the Mary Cady Tew Memorial Fund.

Yale University Press books may be purchased in quantity for educational,
business, or promotional use. For information, please e-mail
sales.press@yale.edu (U.S. office) or sales@yaleup.co.uk (U.K. office).

Set in Janson Roman type by Integrated Publishing Solutions.
Printed in the United States of America.

Library of Congress Control Number: 2020946716
ISBN 978-0-300-25125-8 (hardcover : alk. paper)

A catalogue record for this book is available from the British Library.

This paper meets the requirements of ANSI/NISO Z39.48-1992
(Permanence of Paper).

10 9 8 7 6 5 4 3 2

Contents

Contents

Acknowledgments

As a proud father of four, I am familiar with the term "it takes a village" to raise children. I now understand that the phrase applies to writing a book as well. For this project, I am indebted to many mentors, colleagues, and friends.

In this book, I seek to reflect lessons drawn from observing President Barack Obama's intellectual rigor in internal policy debates on China, as well as his clear and forthright approach to dealing with difficult challenges with Chinese leaders. The book also is informed by my good fortune in having access to—and extended conversations with—central participants in the American policy-making process. I am deeply grateful to Susan Rice for including me in her thinking, planning, and travels on issues relating to China. I feel fortunate to have had many opportunities to join masters of their craft in their engagements with Chinese counterparts, including Bill Burns, John Kerry, Tony Blinken, Avril Haines, Jon Huntsman, and Gary Locke. I owe a debt of gratitude to Evan Medeiros for hiring me to join the National Security Council staff and to Dan Kritenbrink for demonstrating what can be accomplished through grit, force of will, kindness, and diplomatic acumen. I learned a lot—and had a lot of fun—working alongside Susan Thornton, Abe Denmark, and Dave Stilwell on China policy. None of my experiences dealing with China would have been possible without Tom Christensen and Ford Hart shoehorning me into a political reporting officer position in the Embassy of the United States, Beijing, many moons ago. I also am indebted to countless scholars and officials in the United States and China who enlightened me about aspects of the bilateral relationship but are not willing or able to be acknowledged by name.

My work here is an attempt to build on the foundations that have been laid by many people I am fortunate to call mentors. Among the many mentors who have informed my views, few stand out more than Jeff Bader, Ken Lieberthal, J. Stapleton Roy, Doug Paal, Tom Christensen, and Bob Goldberg. Although they all bring their own style to their dealings with Chinese counterparts, they all are brutally effective in eliciting information and emphasizing their views with Chinese interlocutors.

No book is the product of a single individual's work. I appreciate the advice and assistance I received in both research and refinement. I benefited from a richness of research support for various aspects of the book, including from Kevin Dong, James Haynes, Zach Balin, Rachel Lambert, and Sarah Ko. Brookings scholar Bruce Jones did more than anyone to make it possible for me to write this book. Two Brookings senior fellows, Cheng Li and Richard Bush, provided valuable guidance at every step in the process. Brookings director of research in foreign policy Michael O'Hanlon offered tremendous advice and perspective on all aspects of the book. Kevin Nealer, principal in the Scowcroft Group, helped me ground my thinking in practical reality and made the process of doing so a lot of fun. My agent, Bridget Matzie, made an idea a reality with her brash clarity on what needed to be done. The team at Yale University Press was remarkably helpful. It included Jaya Chatterjee, Eva Skewes, Mary Pasti, Sonia Shannon, Aldo Cupo, and Dustin Kilgore.

Most importantly, I thank my wife, Meredith Sumpter, and my children, Helen, Reed, Byron, and Henry, for their unquestioning support. Embarking on this project would not have been possible without them. They are the anchor of my world, the loves of my life, and the ones to whom I dedicate this book.

Introduction

The United States and China stand today at the greatest inflection point in their relations since they established diplomatic ties in 1979. Neither side feels satisfied with the current relationship. Washington and Beijing both seek to revise how each side relates to the other and how both countries relate to the rest of the world. A broadly continuous U.S. policy orientation of the last several decades that seeks to deliver a blend of cooperation and competition—with a focus on maximizing the former and managing the latter so as to prevent escalation to conflict—has come to feel unsatisfactory to many Americans. Such dissatisfactions have become more charged as anger has built over losses in lives and economic opportunities resulting from COVID-19, a pandemic that originated in China and that a segment of the American population blames Chinese authorities for not doing a better job of halting. The U.S.-China relationship has come to be defined by overheated rhetoric, simmering antagonism, and intense distrust. President Trump and others have convinced many Americans that they are being disadvantaged by a flawed relationship that favors China at the expense of the United States.

The rising heat around China in the United States has real-world implications. In addition to foreclosing any capacity for U.S.-China coordination on shared threats, rising antagonism is fueling a sense of urgency in Washington to blunt China's rise. The United States has launched sweeping unilateral tariffs against China, triggering a predictable retaliatory response from Beijing. Even as we have seen a truce on escalation in the trade war at the time of this writing, the two nations have made no progress in resolving any of the structural sources of tension in the trade relationship. China continues to distort global markets with preferential treatment for its own firms. Meanwhile, technological competition is steadily intensifying as both countries seek to limit their own vulnerabilities while also working to dull the other side's comparative advantages. The United States has tightened export controls to limit sales of high-tech products to Chinese firms, and China has sought to gain advantage over the United States in setting global standards.

America's efforts to weaken China are harming itself. Two years of the trade war forced the United States Treasury to spend $28 billion in farm subsidies to partially offset the losses to the American agricultural sector. By point of comparison, this amount is twice what America spent a decade earlier to bail out its auto industry during the great recession. The financial costs will not be limited to the $28 billion, though. China has likely been permanently lost as a reliable agricultural export market for American growers. Outside of agriculture, major American corporations such as Apple and Ford have cited China trade tensions as striking blows to their bottom lines. Boeing has not sold a single plane to China since the trade war began. These firms are far from alone, though, since S&P 500 firms derive on average between one-third and one-half of their profits from China. Major American semiconductor and chip makers have warned that they will need to slash their own research and development budgets if they can no longer generate revenue from sales to China. Partly to hedge against these risks, a number of American high-tech firms have begun offshoring research and development so as to avoid *de minimis* product origin requirements that could trigger export control regulations that would impair their ability to sell products to China in the future. Ironically, even President Trump has complained that the Department of Defense's rising budget requests to counter the China challenge have been crowding out government funding for domestic priorities, like infrastructure.

The longer the United States runs down this counterproductive path of unilaterally pressuring Beijing in hopes that doing so will compel China to change, the more America will drain its own sources of strength. No other country in the world is following the United States in adopting a posture of omnidirectional confrontation. In addition to distancing the United States from its allies and partners on China issues, this approach is leading the United States and China to find fewer areas of cooperation, more areas of confrontation, and diminishing capacity for managing tensions. Even after the outbreak of COVID-19, a threat to humanity that in ordinary circumstances would compel the United States and China to come together to exercise leadership in fashioning a coordinated international response, both countries have been unable to find common cause. Their failure to do so will cause lasting harm to both countries, both in their international image and in their inability to protect their own citizens from a global pandemic. In short, the United States is pursuing a losing strategy that will leave it more isolated from friends and more impotent in influencing China's choices the longer it is pursued.

This book is designed to light a path for a more constructive approach to responding to China's rise. My argument here is anchored in a judgment that managing China's rise as a peer competitor poses the most direct test of American foreign policy in decades.

Introduction

Our present moment demands detailed discussion of the policy choices facing the United States and its allies and partners, as well as an honest accounting of the trade-offs of various options. What objectives and assumptions should guide U.S. policy? What are China's ambitions, both in relation to the United States and for China's role in the world? What is the distribution of power between the United States and China, and between both nations and the rest of the world? Can America's leading firms out-innovate their Chinese competitors, particularly when Chinese firms are advantaged by state backing? How real is the risk of U.S.-China conflict? What is the objective of American strategy with respect to relations with other major powers? And how can the United States maximally secure its interests in the face of growing competition from China?

Long-term structural changes in the power dynamics between Washington and Beijing are not a passing phenomenon but rather a new feature of competition that is here to stay. The United States and China are racing ahead of everyone else in wealth, power, and prestige, and the gap between them and every other country in the world is likely to widen in the years to come. At the same time, competition between the United States and China is intensifying.

Even so, no immutable diplomatic laws of gravity determine that intensifying competition between a rising power and an established power will lead to conflict. Indeed, both the United States and China have strong incentives to avoid conflict, given the catastrophic consequences that would flow to both countries, and indeed the world economy, if such a scenario were ever to materialize.

To understand the nature of U.S.-China relations, I propose the concept of competitive interdependence. Competition is the principal feature, and the costs of breaking free of interdependence are prohibitive. Neither country is capable of imposing its will on the other at acceptable cost or risk, and yet both countries hold preferences and priorities that place them at sharp odds with each other

4

on fundamental issues, ranging from the balance between social stability versus individual liberties to the role of the state in the economy and the distribution of power in the international system. Given these dynamics, as well as the discontinuities in China's actions at home and abroad, the old policy playbook for managing U.S.-China relations no longer holds answers for the challenges that China's rise poses to America and its place in the world.

I intend this book to provide practical recommendations for how the United States can best update its strategy to protect and advance its interests in the face of China's rise. I also seek to right-size the scale of the challenges that China poses to American interests. I urge policy makers to remain vigilant against what former defense secretary James Schlesinger euphemistically described during the Cold War as "ten-foot-tall syndrome," wherein the United States convinced itself that its Soviet competitors were towering figures of immense strength and overwhelming intellect.[1] Exaggerating China's strengths creates anxiety. Anxiety generates insecurity, insecurity leads to overreaction, and overreaction produces bad decisions that undermine America's own competitiveness.

Much of America's anxiety about China's rise is induced by China's rapid economic growth. The American economy was nearly ten times larger than China's in 2000. In 2006, shortly before the global financial crisis, the U.S. economy was still more than five times the size of China's. Now, by contrast, the American economy is roughly 35 percent larger than China's.

The United States' current bout of anxiety about its ability to outpace China is not a new phenomenon. The United States is going through at least its sixth cycle of declinist fears since the 1950s, following similar episodes after *Sputnik*, Soviet expansionism in the 1960s, the OPEC oil embargo of 1973, the U.S. defeat in Vietnam, and the surge in Japanese economic growth in the 1980s. As in past cycles, strong voices inside the United States are sounding the alarm about America's weaknesses and China's ambitions to seize global leadership at America's expense. But Samuel Huntington's insight from 1988 still rings true today: "Declinists may be a better indicator of American psychology than of American power."[2]

The United States need not—and should not—seek to stand in China's way and turn China into an enemy in the process. Instead the United States should approach its relationship with China from a position of confidence that is born of America's considerable assets and advantages. Such confidence in America's strengths relative to China should enable the United States to pursue a steady and affirmative strategy with China that matches capabilities to aspirations and contains clarity on objectives and consistency in pursuit of them.

The goal of American strategy should be to channel China's rise in the direction of being ambitious without growing aggressive, toward either the United States or its security partners. By concentrating on its own progress, the United States should aim to outpace China in economic innovation and outshine it in delivering better governance to its people. The United States has a fundamental interest in preserving the credibility of its security commitments, protecting its open access to Asia, upholding a dynamic international order that is anchored in adherence to accepted rules and norms, and preventing great power conflict. U.S. interests would also be served by urging China to assume a greater burden in addressing global challenges. U.S. values demand that America continue to prioritize efforts to push China's leaders to become more responsive to the needs and rights of their citizens. And it remains critical to America's standing in the world that its leading companies gain greater access to China's slowing but still growing market. To be durable, this approach will also need to deliver benefits to both shareholders and workers.

These objectives remain eminently achievable, even amid current circumstances in the United States and the global effects of the COVID-19 pandemic and in the face of China's rise. Attaining these objectives would ensure that the United States maintains its strong leadership position in the international system, a vibrant economy, and access to the fastest-growing region of the world.

Throughout the book, I lay out my case for why these goals should guide American policy, and how the nation could pursue them most effectively. I argue that the United States holds significant comparative advantages over China, which should give the United States confidence to concentrate more on nurturing its own sources of strength and less on defensively seeking to blunt China's progress. America cannot choose China's path; America can only control its own.

In examining China's strategic ambitions, I argue that Beijing has long aspired to restore China to its self-perceived historical position as the preeminent power in Asia and a central actor on the world stage. Beijing would also like to dim the attraction of liberal norms of democracy and to normalize China's governance practices. I argue that even as many of Beijing's ambitions are in tension with American interests and values, nothing is preordained about China's ability to achieve its goals. To constrain the export of more malign aspects of China's system, the United States will need to tighten coordination with like-minded friends. Most of all, though, the United States will need to rediscover how to inspire others through the power of its own example.

I introduce the concept of competitive interdependence as the framework for understanding the nature of U.S.-China relations. A shared acceptance by Washington and Beijing of this framework would help to limit competition and reduce direct challenges to each other's vital interests, not out of amity but rather out of clear-eyed recognition that both sides need to maintain an ability to co-exist within a heightened state of competition.

In examining the nature of technological and economic competition between the United States and China, I observe that the United States is repeating a historical pattern of growing insecure about its ability to compete against a state-guided model for scientific innovation. I explain why only China will be able to slow China down, and only America will determine its own future course. The sooner the United States diagnoses and fixes its own domestic shortcomings that are hobbling its progress, the sooner it will be able to lower its anxieties about China's advances and focus instead on strengthening its own competitiveness.

China's rapid advances in military capabilities and its concentration of forces along its maritime periphery have ushered in an end to U.S. military primacy in East Asia. Both countries are now locked in an intensifying security dilemma. To manage this dilemma and avoid tripping into conflict, both sides will need to isolate and manage areas of competition with the greatest potential to trigger conflict. Rather than search for an elusive grand bargain, both sides should commit to pursuing practical and incremental ways to solve specific problems, for instance, by drawing inspiration from the U.S.-Soviet record of risk reduction during the Cold War. At the same time, the United States will need to strengthen its ability to deter problematic Chinese behavior, for instance by updating its force posture and its overall defense concept against China.

I argue that American foreign policy should no longer strive to reconstitute a form of *Pax Americana*, whereby the United States serves as the central power broker in every region of the world, but rather pursue balances of power that favor American interests. If the United States can meet this condition, then other major powers—with the exception of Russia—will naturally be guided by shared interests and values with the United States to coordinate efforts with Washington for managing specific challenges posed by China's behavior. Washington will need to resist impulses to insist that the European Union, India, and Japan align with the United States in opposition to China, and instead patiently allow such coordination to develop on an issue-by-issue basis in instances when interests align.

Introduction

In contemplating how best to respond to this new distribution of power in the international system where the United States is no longer the preeminent power in every region, I argue that policy makers must resist the easy allure of "great power competition" as the organizing principle of American foreign policy. Binary "good versus evil" approaches risk generating strategic costs for the United States in misallocated resources, deepening divisions with allies on China, and intensifying enmity with Beijing that would exceed anticipated benefits. Rather, to attract international support and domestic buy-in for an affirmative strategy of outcompeting China, the United States will need to develop a confident strategy that is capable not only of deterring problematic Chinese behavior but also of inviting greater Chinese contributions to addressing global challenges. America's future prosperity and security will be determined principally by its own decisions and actions. That is where the United States must concentrate its focus.

The thread tying these chapters together is an argument that the United States is still the stronger power in the U.S.-China relationship and will remain so as long as it nurtures its sources of comparative advantage. The more the United States can preserve confidence in its societal and governance models, the better it will be able to focus attention where it matters most: not on slowing China down, but rather on strengthening itself. To compete effectively with China, America's leaders should focus on fostering greater national cohesion, restoring America's international prestige, and preserving its historically unmatched network of alliance relationships. These are keys to America's competitiveness that China does not have and cannot take away from the United States.

Some might counter that Beijing poses such a dire threat, with ambitions so antithetical to American interests, that Washington must derail China's rise now while America still maintains material advantages. Others may argue that China has earned America's enmity through its latent hostility and its fundamental unfairness toward the United States. Still others may see China's behavior, particularly its abuse of the rights of its own people, as so abhorrent as to demand an outraged American response. Many in the United States also argue that China should be leveraged as an external threat to unite a fractured country, much as the Soviet Union served to dull partisan divisions at key moments during the Cold War.

I am sympathetic to many of these arguments. I agree that China poses the most potent challenge to America's place in the world since the end of the Cold War. Having dealt up close with China's leaders for the better part of the past decade, I am fully aware of the tensely competitive nature of the relationship, and of the animus that many Chinese officials ascribe to American actions and intentions. I readily acknowledge China's revisionist ambitions, particularly those directed at coercing Taiwan's twenty-three million residents to abandon their democratic principles and accept unification with the mainland. I reject arguments that China has benign ambitions or that it can be pacified through accommodation. I recognize China's drive to dilute the universal reach of values that I, as an American diplomat, determinedly sought to advance. As the former U.S. Embassy political reporting officer for Xinjiang, I am strongly affected by China's repression there. I also see plainly the unfair nature of China's state-led mercantilist economic model and its impacts on hardworking Americans.

Even so, outrage is an ineffective emotion for managing relations among great powers. Relations between powers such as the United States and China seldom lend themselves to grand public breakthroughs or triumphs of good over evil. Successful outcomes are often measured by crises averted and steps taken in the direction of American interests and values. Assumptions that American pressure can compel Chinese capitulation are built on a dangerous level of ignorance about the limits of American leverage, and on willful disregard of Chinese leaders' incentives to avoid the humiliation of appearing to be pushed around by the United States. No

Chinese leader will allow a perception to emerge of bowing in the face of visible American pressure. And no one-sided agreement reached under duress will outlive the Chinese leader who acceded to it.

Instead, the United States will need to be clear-eyed about how best to protect and advance its interests with China. The more China gains in wealth, prestige, and power, the more necessary it will be for the United States to coordinate with other allies and partners to influence how China identifies and pursues its interests. America's ability to attract international support for its efforts to influence China's choices will rest on consistent demonstrations of steadiness and confidence. Washington must show that its actions are informed by an awareness of the interests of its partners, and that it is pursuing a strategy that will sustain beyond turnovers in administration. Demonstrating the durability of such an approach, in turn, will require the United States to coalesce around a strategy that reflects the level of prioritization and pain tolerance that the American people place on China. For most Americans, China simply is not a central preoccupation or concern. Even as the American public shows broad and rising dissatisfaction with Chinese behavior, most Americans do not identify China as a top threat to the United States and do not support shouldering significant sacrifices in service of confrontation with China.[3]

In sum, my goal for this book is straightforward. It is not partisan. The challenges I seek to grapple with are far bigger than the Trump administration. This book is designed to address hard questions about how the United States can most effectively secure its interests as China solidifies itself as the second-largest power and nearest peer competitor to the United States in the international system.

My hope is that the book sparks a healthy debate about how the United States can most effectively manage China's rise, including by thinking clearly about where the United States should prioritize efforts for responding to China's actions and ambitions. Although I suggest ways in which the United States could adapt its approach to China, nothing would make me happier than to see these recommendations improved on by others going forward. Managing China's rise effectively will be a generational challenge. It is not a project that lends itself to easy or absolute answers. But some ideas and impulses are better than others.

Even with China's surge in strength, the United States still holds a stronger hand than China. Now America must play its cards well.

ONE

America's Enduring Strengths

In the comparison of national power between the United States and China, the United States remains dominant by a sizable margin, retaining abundant capacity to protect its vital interests even as China continues its rise. The United States need not—and should not—seek to block China's rise and in the process turn China into an adversary. Rather, the United States should get back to playing offense, concentrating on strengthening its own ability to outpace China economically and outshine China in its capacity to unlock the potential of its people.

Setting the Context

Over the course of his presidential campaigns in 2016 and 2020, Donald Trump nursed countless grievances—grievances designed to help Americans assign blame to others for the frustrations they were feeling. Few complaints carried as much weight as the ones he reserved for China, though. In his telling, China was the chief culprit for American job losses and economic malaise, and the cause of American suffering as a result of COVID-19.

Trump's critique found most direct expression during the 2016 campaign at a concert-like campaign rally in Fort Wayne, Indiana, where he told a raucous crowd, "We can't continue to allow China to rape our country, and that's what they're doing."[1] The crowd roared back their satisfaction. Ever eager to perfect an applause line, Trump spent the rest of the 2016 campaign building on that theme, blaming his predecessors for being too "weak" to counter the challenge and promising that he alone would "fix" problems with China. A similar pattern of toughness versus weakness guided Trump's messaging on China during the 2020 campaign.

Trump won the 2016 election by a razor-thin margin. The contest hinged on Pennsylvania, Ohio, Michigan, and Wisconsin, and within those four states, the balance swung in large part on the votes of working-class white voters.[2] It was at these voters that Trump aimed his message on China. He used populist, protectionist rhetoric to show that he was different, that he was willing to break crockery and do whatever it took to defend hardworking Americans. His unapologetically aggressive posture on China likely contributed to his narrow electoral win in 2016.

I watched Trump's daily China bashing closely throughout 2016 from my office at the White House, where I was serving as China director on the National Security Council staff for President Barack Obama. Even before the votes were counted, Trump's incendiary remarks were already having an impact on the U.S.-China relationship. Many in Beijing had long assumed that as the gap in national power between China and the United States shrank, the United States would grow increasingly wary of China and more determined to suppress its rise. They saw Trump as an embodiment of their expectations. But few Chinese officials with whom I interacted expected that moment to arrive so soon or so sharply. They began to ask me privately, "Why is the United States losing its confidence? Are Americans really that anxious about China's rise?"

Around a month after the dust from the 2016 presidential election had settled, I found myself at Trump Tower to deliver a transition briefing to the leadership of the incoming National Security Council team. I was responsible, along with two colleagues, for sharing the logic and assumptions that guided the Obama administration's China policy, and the successes and shortcomings of the approach undertaken. While I felt duty bound to prepare the new team as best I could, I also felt a nagging curiosity to learn if president-elect Trump's rhetoric on China was primarily political posturing or if it reflected deeply held convictions. My curiosity was quelled five minutes into the briefing when a top official in Trump's transition team interrupted our presentation to say that he had heard enough. The Obama administration's "problem," he said, was that we did not appreciate that the United States was locked in an existential battle with China, and if the United States did not "win" and "defeat" China, the very existence of the United States as we know it could soon be in doubt. The incoming team said it knew what it needed to know about China, and after a short period of small talk about the upcoming Army-Navy football game, the briefing came to an abrupt and awkward close.

I left Trump Tower disoriented. I wondered how the world's preeminent power, with the most capable fighting force, the strongest network of allies, and the largest economy in history, could come to feel so vulnerable to losing everything to a rising power that lagged considerably behind in virtually every metric of national power.

I knew these would not just be academic questions. After all the hype from the election, the new administration would need to demonstrate that it was breaking with the past and taking a new approach to countering China. And it did.

The new team quickly jettisoned a practice spanning six previous administrations of working in close consultation with America's allies and partners to influence Beijing's behavior. Instead the Trump administration began from the premise that U.S. and Chinese interests are irreconcilably in conflict with each other, that China's rise would continue ineluctably into the future unless the United States impeded it, and that China's gains equated to American losses. From this framework, the defining question for policy makers moved from how most effectively to manage relations with a rising power to how to slow (and, if possible, stop) China's advances. Although one could point to considerable differences between how President Trump and members of his administration spoke about China, and indeed between how leaders in each department and agency discussed the matter, there was one common touchstone: where others before them had been weak, the Trump administration would be strong. Differentiating itself from the Obama administration became the best predictor for anticipating the Trump administration's policy decisions on China.

In its inaugural National Security Strategy, the Trump administration revived language to discuss China that had previously been reserved for the Soviet Union during the Cold War. The document characterized China as a revisionist power seeking to "erode American security and prosperity," and as a country with which the United States is locked in a contest between freedom and repression. Just two years earlier, in the 2015 National Security Strategy, the United States had welcomed "the rise of a stable, peaceful, and prosperous China" and expressed an aspiration "to develop a constructive relationship with China that delivers benefits for our two peoples and promotes security and prosperity in Asia and around the world."

Thus, in the span of twenty-four months, the official policy of the United States shifted from viewing China as a potential partner with whom it would need to manage critical differences to an entrenched rival that seeks to harm the United States. Rarely, if ever before, has U.S. policy on an issue of such strategic significance shifted so sharply in such a short period and in the absence of any form of militarized conflict.

A Changed China

To be sure, China did change in the two years between 2015 and 2017. Under President Xi Jinping, the country became more aggressive at home and abroad. Xi boldly and unapologetically made clear his desire for China to reclaim its historical mantle as a leader on the world stage and a central actor in regional affairs. Xi's invocation of China's global ambitions, encompassing an ambiguous but evident military component, fed concerns about intensifying U.S.-China geostrategic competition.

China's newfound assertiveness under President Xi was a departure from China's recent past. Previously, China had been unique for its self-awareness and restraint. Arguably more so than any other rising power in the past several centuries, China seemed to have internalized the importance of not raising alarm about its rise.

Leaders in Beijing had studied Germany's experience under Bismarck of patiently unifying the country and amassing strength. They understood the calamities that befell Germany when Wilhelm II decided it was time for Germany to stand up and assert itself outside the shadow of Great Britain. They similarly understood Japan's experience after the Meiji Restoration, where caution gave way to impatience and ultimately resulted in Japan's defeat to the Allied powers in World War II.[3] They studied the Soviet Union's "mistake" of entering a universalistic ideological struggle with the United States during the Cold War, and the ruinous results that followed.

Aware of these historical precedents, former paramount leader Deng Xiaoping and other leaders who followed placed China on a steady course of gradually reforming its economy, opening to the outside world, seeking to preserve a generally stable periphery, and avoiding collisions with the United States. These were elements of the formula that helped fuel China's historical rise from an economic backwater to a global power in the span of several decades.

In recent years, though, Deng's formula has given way to a more impatient and nationalistic assertion of China's rising role in the international system. Xi has stoked Chinese national pride by taking an uncompromising position on territorial disputes and building a strong military force to assert China's claims. China has constructed seven artificial islands on contested rocks and submerged features in the South China Sea, leading many in the United States to conclude that such efforts are a precursor to a Chinese push to establish an exclusive sphere of influence in East Asia. Xi launched the most ambitious international development program of the twenty-first century—the Belt and Road Initiative—to build trading routes between China and the rest of the world. He established new Chinese-led international institutions, such as the Asian Infrastructure Investment Bank (AIIB), that appeared to seek to displace existing Western-led institutions. And unlike previous leaders, Xi demonstrated greater tolerance for friction with the United States in pursuit of China's national ambitions. That many of these decisions were made before Xi's assumption of power, and indeed trace back to judgments Beijing made about its strategic environment around the time of the global financial crisis in 2008 and 2009,[4] did not diminish a prevailing view within the Trump administration that Beijing was stealing a march on Washington and needed to be stopped.

Xi also reasserted the Chinese Communist Party's role at the center of all issues within China. In so doing, he extinguished any lingering hopes for political reform, shrank space for dissent, suppressed voices calling for change, and, in the most egregious example of heavy-handedness, locked up at least one million—and maybe more—ethnic Uighurs in Xinjiang under the guise of "reeducation." Beijing also curtailed space for uncensored media, tightened restrictions on foreign nongovernmental organizations, and constructed a sweeping surveillance architecture across the country.

Xi also scrapped presidential (and vice presidential) term limits, signaling his intention to stay in power beyond the end of his second term in 2023. Xi's power play, paired with Putin's own political actions in Russia and the ascent of strongmen in Turkey, Hungary, and elsewhere, has raised alarm bells about an oncoming era of digitally empowered authoritarianism.[5]

In other words, China's increasing assertiveness abroad and illiberalism at home have undoubtedly played a role in America's policy shift. But Chinese actions alone do not explain the sharpness of America's turn. Other factors have also been at play.

Disappointment in Chinese Reform

One element driving the bitterness toward China has been a broadly held sense of unmet expectations in the United States about China's political and economic reform. President Clinton embodied America's peak optimism about changing China. In debates about China's accession to the World Trade Organization, Clinton famously argued that economic opening would lead to political reform in China. Although American strategy generally was not guided by gauzy hopes of economic progress leading arithmetically to an outbreak of electoral democracy in China, such hopes were no doubt stoked in the minds of the public through overexuberant rhetoric by American officials.[6]

Economic expansion has strengthened the legitimacy of an oppressive authoritarian system in China and reinforced an instinct in Beijing to stick with what works—for example, leveraging market access to compel technology transfer, and maintaining state involvement in strategic industries through subsidized state-owned enterprises. As the Office of the United States Trade Representative has documented, "This heavy state role in the economy, reinforced by unchecked discretionary actions of Chinese regulators, has generated serious trade frictions with China's many trade partners, including the United States."[7] These frictions have been amplified by a broadly held resentment in the United States that China's unfair economic policies have been fueling China's rapid economic rise at a time when many Americans have been experiencing stagnant wages and diminishing opportunities for economic advancement.

A Growing Sense of Vulnerability

When Donald Trump rouses audiences by bashing China, he is not simply tapping into their disappointment. He is stirring their fear. Fear is born of insecurity, and insecurity is in full supply in many communities across the United States. More and more Americans feel as though they are working harder only to fall further behind, deeper into a debt they fear they will never be able to pay off.

A growing body of public polling illustrates the sense of malaise many Americans are feeling.[8] Faith in the American Dream is fading. Economic mobility is declining as more opportunities flow to those at the top of the social ladder. According to a study by the labor economist Tom Hertz, only one out of every one hundred children born into the poorest fifth of households, and fewer than one out of every fifty children born into the middle fifth, will join the top 5 percent of earners.[9]

Even before the economic calamity induced by COVID-19, the United States was already going through a period of transition every bit as disruptive as the Industrial Revolution. Entire industries were becoming obsolete, and working-class Americans were getting pummeled. Roughly 7.5 million manufacturing jobs have been lost since China began its policy of reform and opening.[10] Although recent research indicates that 85 percent of manufacturing job losses are attributable to technological change—largely automation—rather than international trade, the feeling generated within a broad segment of American society remains the same: fear, helplessness, and frustration.[11]

The wave of change for the American workforce is still building, not receding. The scale of job losses in the United States that will result from the adoption of artificial intelligence, automation, and robotics in the coming years is staggering. This shift could be accelerated by COVID-19 as more companies search for efficiencies to minimize costs during a down market. A team of researchers at the Organisation for Economic Co-operation and Development found that 10 percent of jobs in the United States are at high risk of being automated—and this is the low end of the spectrum of predictions of job losses.[12] More alarmingly, former treasury secretary Larry Summers has calculated that the rise of AI adoption could bring about unemployment for about one-third of American men ages twenty-five to fifty-four by midcentury. And the renowned technologist Kai-Fu Lee predicts that within ten to twenty years, the United States will technologically be capable of automating between 40 and 50 percent of jobs.[13]

On top of these economic changes, America's society is undergoing an unprecedented demographic transition. Experts now predict that the United States will become majority minority by 2045 as the white population ages and the combined racial minority population continues to expand. This shift already is nearing a tipping point among younger age groups: minorities now outnumber whites among youth under eighteen.[14] These dramatic socioeconomic and demographic changes have created fertile ground for populism and nationalism to sprout.

Fear of America Falling Behind

These economic and demographic shifts are jolting American society and triggering anxieties about America losing ground to China. Against this backdrop, many Americans are energized by reminders of the United States as "number one," and of America as the indispensable global power.

President Trump appears to grasp this need for projections of confidence. He recognizes that even though many Americans feel insecure about their own prospects, they find reassurance in pronouncements of America's strength. By contrast, President Obama's foreign policy, while arguably strong on the merits, in many ways fell flat for people desiring to be reminded of America's dominance.

President Obama was guided by a dispassionate judgment—correct, in my view—that the United States would need to learn to wean itself from an impulse to believe it could do whatever it wanted, whenever it wanted, wherever it wanted. He did not subscribe to the view that every international problem had an American solution, just as he also did not believe that vital American interests were implicated in every overseas crisis. To retain maximal influence in a modern, globalized world, he believed, the United States would need to exercise restraint in where and how it involved itself in other countries' affairs.

Obama accepted that China would rise, and as it did so, it would seek more of a leadership role on the world stage. He was comfortable with a highly competitive relationship with China. As I learned from firsthand experience, Obama also was perfectly fine with piercingly direct exchanges with Xi Jinping. Neither Obama nor Xi expressed any displeasure or elevated emotion during such exchanges; both understood that "business was business." They both also seemed to appreciate that neither was needy toward the other, either in personal temperament or in the nature of the requests they made. They both also understood that their word was the currency by which each would measure the other.

Obama also believed that a capable China that contributed more to addressing global challenges would relieve a burden on the United States. He also judged that America's ability to address many of the most vexing transnational challenges it confronted—pandemic diseases, nuclear proliferation, climate change, food security—would be enhanced if China was pulling in the same direction. For the most part, Obama sought to wall off China policy from politics, which by its very nature prioritizes short-term calculations and appealing to the passions of the moment. While I viewed this approach as wise and self-aware, many Americans, I have learned, did not. Where I saw wisdom, others saw weakness.

The Shifting Political Landscape

Virtually every major constituency in American politics with a stake in U.S.-China relations now holds a jaundiced view of China's behavior. Increasingly within the United States, China's gains are viewed as America's losses. President Trump and his team have built a narrative around China as a rival: a country that cheats, cannot be trusted, and represents a worldview at odds with American values.[15] China policy itself has become politicized. China is a stock feature of President Trump's daily tweets and public remarks. Trump has sought to popularize a view that China's perfidy is the root cause of the pain many Americans feel from the ravages of the COVID-19 pandemic. In such circumstances, there are no points to be scored for compromise. There are only winners and losers.

The problem with such a zero-sum approach is that diplomacy between great powers is rarely ever conducted in a binary win-lose fashion. U.S.-China relations are no exception. Furthermore, when victory is not a plausible outcome and compromise is equated with weakness, then dramatizing the threat becomes the last politically viable option. Beijing has largely responded in kind, wielding its propaganda apparatus to drum up anti-American sentiment, and a vicious cycle has taken hold. Both countries are being swept forward in the emerging great power rivalry by a rising tide of nationalism. This is a pox on both houses.

Exaggerating China's Strengths, Overlooking Its Weaknesses

In recent years, the United States has fixated on China's strengths and failed to take account of America's competitive advantages. This has led Washington to adopt a lopsidedly adversarial policy orientation that is fueling U.S.-China enmity. It has also distracted American focus from addressing its own shortcomings at home.

To be clear, Beijing's behavior has been the principal contributor to the downturn in U.S.-China relations. I spent the better part of the past decade warning Chinese officials that failure to address America's serious and growing concerns on issues such as intellectual property theft, cybersecurity, human rights, and militarization of the South China Sea would eventually push the relationship into a downward spiral. My prediction has been borne out. Even so, the core question confronting policy makers must be not whether the United States has justification for feeling righteous in its indignation but rather how the United States should respond to Chinese actions in a way that maximally pushes China in America's preferred direction.

China has shed its past modesty in favor of a newfound bravado to assert itself as number one. Through its "Made in China 2025" plan, China has declared its intention to dominate industries of the future. Its "New Generation Artificial Intelligence Development Plan" asserts that China will become the leading AI power by 2030. Its stated ambitions for the Belt and Road Initiative, and for its military modernization, are no less grand.

The pace of China's economic expansion has lent credibility to these bold objectives. Even with a 4.5 percent drop in the rate of GDP growth from 2010 to 2019,[16] China added the rough equivalent of Australia's economy to its own in 2018,[17] making China the largest engine of global economic expansion.[18] The sustained pace of growth over more than three decades has caused many to accept that China's rocket ride will continue well into the future.

It is not just words or statistics that are stoking anxieties. In recent decades, China has also poured significant resources into its military. China today has the world's second-largest defense budget, the world's largest conventional missile force, and the largest navy

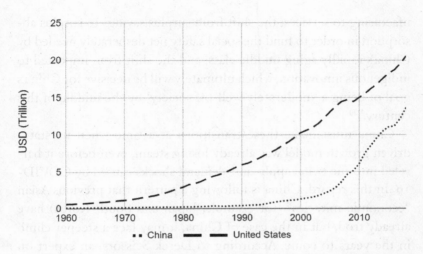

Nominal U.S.-China GDP growth, 1960–2018 (current GDP)
Data from World Bank

and coast guard by counts of hulls. These investments have given China military supremacy over many of its neighbors, an ability to raise the level of risk to the United States if it chose to challenge China in regional disputes, and a growing—though still limited—capacity to project power outward from its coastal waters.[19]

As impressive as China's rise has been, we have real reasons to interrogate assumptions that this trajectory will continue indefinitely in the future. Beneath its veneer of bristling strength, China also faces serious vulnerabilities.

Stalling Economic Reform

China confronts major challenges as it seeks to transition to a more sustainable long-term economic growth model. As the former chairman of Morgan Stanley Asia and Yale University professor Stephen Roach has put it, China must make four transitions: "the shift from export- and investment-led growth to an economy driven increasingly by domestic private consumption; the shift from manufacturing to services; the shift from surplus savings to surplus absorption in order to fund the social safety net desperately needed by China's rapidly aging middle class; and the shift from imported to indigenous innovation, which ultimately will be decisive for China's goal of being a 'moderately well-off society' by the middle of this century."[20]

China must make these transitions at a time when its state-driven growth model was already losing steam, even before it barreled into the twin supply-and-demand shocks caused by COVID-19. In this regard, China is following a pattern that previous Asian "economic miracles" (for example, Japan and South Korea) have already trod, but in the case of China, it may face a steeper climb in the years to come. According to Derek Scissors, an expert on China's economy, "Historical comparisons to Japan and Korea across a range of indicators (i.e., personal income, agricultural productivity, labor productivity, return on capital, innovation) show China's miracle has faded prematurely, leaving the country far from rich and with little prospect to become so."[21]

For decades, China's rapid economic rise has been built on a growing labor supply and rapid capital investment in areas such as infrastructure and urbanization that increased efficiencies and enabled greater productivity. Now China is at risk of growing old before it grows rich. Whereas the U.S. median age is projected to remain stable for the rest of the century, China's median age is projected to surge from thirty-five to fifty between 2015 and 2050. China is already beginning to suffer the demographic consequences of its one-child policy. The number of Chinese older than sixty-five is expected to rise from roughly 130 million to 410 million—more than the population of the United States. China will go from having eight workers to cover each retiree in 2019 to two workers per retiree in 2050.[22]

In other words, China's demographic dividend has been depleted. The big shift of labor from rural farms to factories is largely

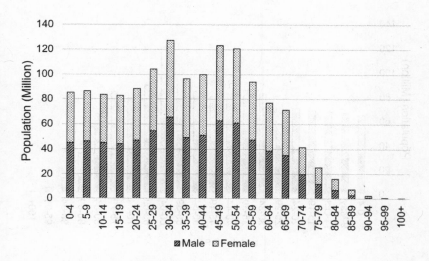

China population by age and gender, 2019
Data from United Nations, Department of Economic and Social Affairs,
Population Division

complete, and the overall population of workers is on a steady down slope. This will place enormous social and economic stress on China's society in coming decades, including by potentially crowding out public spending for nonsocial services like research and development, overseas development financing, and defense. China's gender imbalance—largely the result of individual decisions by families to abort females in favor of males during the period of the nation's one-child policy—will also add stress to the country's social cohesion.

China has also maxed out its credit card at a relatively early stage of its development, before it navigates through the notorious middle-income trap. The middle-income trap is an economic concept that applies to countries such as China that experience rapid economic growth by harnessing cheap labor and capital but later get stuck transitioning to higher value-added economic output based on rising productivity and innovation.

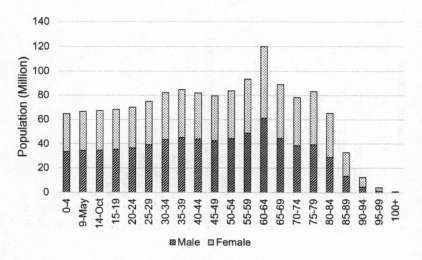

China population by age and gender, 2050
Data from United Nations, Department of Economic and Social Affairs,
Population Division

Rising debt levels will make it harder for China to buy its way up the ladder from low-end manufacturing to high value-added production. As a point of comparison, the Republic of Korea and Taiwan limited public spending at earlier stages of their development, thus preserving space for capital-intensive efforts to push their economic model from low-end production to higher value-added manufacturing as they worked through the middle-income trap.

By contrast, China's debt as a percentage of GDP more than doubled over the last decade, from 141 percent in 2008 to over 300 percent in July 2019.[23] As debt has ballooned, Beijing has relied on its own credibility as a lender of last resort to serve as a bulwark of stability. As China's financial system rapidly expands, though, Beijing's ability to tamp down volatility could come under greater scrutiny. This systemic risk could become more pronounced as China's economy slows and its state-owned enterprises face greater challenges servicing their debt.

The third leg of economic growth, after labor and capital, is productivity. Here, as well, a positive outcome is anything but ensured. China's rate of productivity growth has been slowing for a variety of reasons, among them that China has already squeezed out many of the gains from transitioning to a price-based market economy, expanding educational opportunity, and upgrading its technology.

China's sectoral curbs on foreign competition and firewalls limiting the free flow of information are placing a drag on productivity. So is the fact that state-controlled banks prefer to lend to relatively inefficient state-owned enterprises, instead of to more innovative private-sector firms. As a result, capital is piling up in inefficient corners of the Chinese economy while nimbler private firms are being starved of funds to grow their businesses.[24]

Many smart technocratic economists in China understand these challenges and have plans for overcoming them, but their voices are increasingly being stifled by pressure to remain politically in line, for example by supporting calls for enhancing the state-driven development model, with the Communist Party playing a central role. So long as political space for economic reform remains limited, China will continue to be challenged to generate productivity growth.

Overall, China's nominal GDP growth rate is slowing considerably and will very likely continue to do so in the coming years. At the same time, even as it cools, the economy is still growing from a large base. China's economy is poised to continue expanding, albeit at a decelerating rate, for the foreseeable future.

A Sclerotic Political System

China's political system is not functioning well. Once renowned for its technocratic competence, the Communist Party is now becoming recognizable for its Leninist rigidity. Key political reforms implemented by Deng to ensure stability and spur innovation have been scrapped under Xi. These include presidential term limits; a distribution of power among the president, premier, and politburo; and a preference for pragmatism over ideological inflexibility. Xi has systematically demolished Deng's political legacy.

Nowadays, propaganda around Xi Jinping and "Xi Jinping Thought" is in overdrive. Mandatory ideological education is becoming increasingly invasive, many economic reforms are stalled, muffled grumbling from the People's Liberation Army about civilian micromanagement is becoming more audible to trained ears, and Xi's signature anticorruption campaign risks opening up rifts within the party. China's slow response to the outbreak of the COVID-19 coronavirus in Wuhan and its focus on censorship over public awareness provide a case study of the flaws of a centralized Leninist political system for addressing incipient crises.

Stress on National Unity

Beijing is also anxious about preserving national cohesion. Part of the Chinese Communist Party's rationale for ruling the country since its inception has been that it is singularly capable of holding China together. This leaves no room for Xi to cede ground, whether on territorial disputes with neighbors or with restive populations in Xinjiang, Tibet, or Hong Kong, to say nothing of Taiwan. This uncompromising ethos for managing regions that Beijing considers to constitute its periphery is generating uniformly bad outcomes from Beijing's perspective; populations in each of these regions are moving away from Beijing and demonstrating greater tolerance for pain in doing so.

Xi's challenges are no less acute on social issues. Beijing's mass incarceration of ethnic Uighurs in Xinjiang, combined with tightening censorship, shrinking space for dissent, repression of civil society, and tightening controls on religious practice, reflects heightened fear and insecurity. These are not signs of a self-confident China aspiring to attract support for enhanced leadership in regional and global affairs.[25]

The Communist Party can no longer rely on the implicit bargain with its population of rapid economic growth in return for one-party rule, given that economic growth rates are slowing. Top leaders have little hope in ideology's ability to play such a role, given the lack of appeal it holds among China's 1.4 billion citizens, even if it does help hold together the ninety million cadres in the Chinese Communist Party. This dilemma is a big part of the reason why Xi Jinping and China's propaganda apparatus spend so much time extolling China's cultural traditions and its civilizational history, in addition to emphasizing a nationwide patriotic education campaign.[26] They view these initiatives as essential for unifying a diverse and dynamic country. As Xi told the Central Committee in 2013, "Winning or losing public support is an issue that concerns the C.P.C.'s survival or extinction."

In the absence of reliably uncensored polling data and the feedback loop of regular elections, China's leaders often lack confidence in their understanding of social forces inside China. Even with its technological advances (for example, its capacity to scrape social media for clues on trends and sources of dissatisfaction), the leadership still does not have a dependable way of receiving public feedback on its own performance. They rely on nationalism and narratives cultivated by the propaganda apparatus to unify a diverse population. And when stoking national honor becomes the safe space politically for China's leaders, policy decisions on contentious issues often skew toward demonstrations of strength and resolve.

Food and Energy Insecurity

China is also confronted with food and energy insecurity. According to Benjamin Shobert, an international health expert, "China's arable land holdings amount to at best 15 percent of its total, with much of this now too contaminated by industrial pollutants to farm. China has 22 percent of the world's population and only 10 percent of the world's arable land."[27] As a consequence, China is food insecure. It depends on stable global markets to meet shortfalls in agricultural commodities needed to feed its people and raise its livestock.

China is also vulnerable in terms of energy security. The country imports roughly half of its oil from the Middle East, and it does not have the naval capacity to protect its sea lines of communication along the entire route. China is establishing naval access facilities along the route from the Middle East to its ports, including a base in Djibouti and other stations in Oman, Pakistan, Sri Lanka, Cambodia, and Myanmar. Even so, in a conflict scenario, China would risk being cut off from its principal suppliers of oil. China recognizes this vulnerability and is working to limit it, including by launching the world's largest renewable-energy program, expanding its network of overland oil pipelines, and increasing its ability to extract from tight shale, but these are projects with time horizons of decades, not years.

Geographic Stresses

China also confronts a uniquely challenging geography. It is bordered by fourteen countries, four of which are nuclear-armed states, and five of which harbor unresolved territorial disputes with Beijing. It risks having regional countries coalesce in challenging China if Beijing seeks to use economic or military muscle to assert a hierarchical leadership role for itself in regional affairs. And unlike the Soviet Union at the end of World War II, which faced power vacuums along its periphery, China is surrounded by a constellation of formidable countries: an aging but wealthy Japan, a rising and nationalistic India, a revanchist Russia, a dynamic and determined Vietnam, a technological front-runner in the Republic of Korea, and a dangerous frenemy in North Korea, just to name a few. All these countries maintain national identities and ambitions that do not involve subordination to China or its interests.

As the regional expert Charles Edel explains, China is relatively hemmed in:

Analysts who portray the competition over who gets to define the rules, norms, and institutions of Asia as divided between China and the United States fall into several traps, including, most prominently, a counting problem. Pitting China's growing naval capabilities against only America's fails to take into account the surface, sub-surface, air, strike, and automated systems its allies and partners collectively bring to bear. For instance, adding in Japan's Maritime Self-Defense Force alone substantially changes the naval balance. . . . Adding in the navies of South Korea, Taiwan, and Australia changes the calculation still further. . . . One could do a similar calculation for airpower, with Japanese and South Korean F-15s regularly training and exercising with the U.S. Air Force. And if one adds in partners like Singapore and India, who are likely to side with America and its allies in a conflict, the balance shifts again. In essence, the Chinese prefer excluding the capabilities of the U.S. alliance system and partners taken together; the Chinese frame it this way to negate the advantages that the United States and its partners hold collectively. To fall for that would be quite stupid for, with it, *a look at the map shows that China is de facto contained as a maritime power.*[28]

Recalling America's Advantages

A sound American policy approach toward China must be capable of weighing China's strengths alongside its weaknesses and also factoring in America's considerable relative advantages. The more that American policy makers can clarify these distinctions, the better they will be able to calibrate U.S. policy responses to Chinese actions, for example by differentiating between Chinese actions that implicate vital American interests and thus merit a strong response and those that do not.

U.S. Alliances

One of the United States' commanding advantages vis-à-vis China is its global network of security alliances and partnerships. The U.S. alliance network encompasses 25 percent of the earth's population and accounts for 75 percent of world GDP and defense spending.[29] This tapestry of alliances and partnerships supports 587 military bases spread across forty-two countries and an American navy and air force stronger than those of the next ten nations combined. According to the Yale historian Paul Kennedy, "Nothing has ever existed like this disparity of power, nothing."[30]

The United States has a record of fighting on behalf of friends and for its values worldwide. The Chinese military does not have experience conducting joint military operations; it last fought against Vietnam in 1979. U.S. leaders have traditionally championed shared values and principles that bind many (though not all) allies with the United States. For all intents and purposes, China does not possess any alliances or relationships that it could rely on for military support in a conflict with the United States. Even the hawkish Chinese international relations scholar Yan Xuetong has acknowledged that Beijing will be unable to compete with the United States on the world stage unless it "develop[s] more high-quality diplomatic and military relationships than Washington."[31]

From a strategic standpoint, China has growing capabilities to concentrate forces and impede America's ability to intervene in a military conflict in East Asia. The U.S. Indo-Pacific Command reports that the People's Liberation Army will reach rough parity with U.S. forces permanently stationed in the Pacific in coming years and eventually surpass them.[32]

But the United States enters this competition from a position of strength. In the event of conflict with China in Asia, the Department of Defense would be able to call on considerable capabilities beyond those solely under the Indo-Pacific Command. America maintains nuclear superiority, as well as strong advantages in undersea warfare and space-based intelligence, surveillance, and reconnaissance capabilities. The United States has an advantage in joint warfighting. Washington also has a more globally dispersed military. This gives the United States greater capacity to protect sea lines of communication and to place stress on Chinese interests outside its immediate periphery. U.S. defense spending remains three times that of China. So while China's growing military creates considerable concern in Washington, America's existing capabilities remain downright intimidating when viewed from Beijing.

International Institutions

Beyond the military sphere, the United States maintains structural advantages in numerous existing international institutions. By dint of its role as principal architect and chief supporter over many decades, Washington plays a predominant role in selecting the leaders of bodies such as the United Nations, the World Bank, and the International Monetary Fund, not to mention countless other regional institutions around the world. This grants the United States significant influence over setting agendas in key international institutions. This advantage has degraded in recent years as the United States has withdrawn from a range of multilateral bodies while China has energetically stepped into the vacuum, but the damage is not yet irreversible.

Innovative Capacity

The United States also boasts the world's most innovative workforce. This advantage has been nurtured by an immigration system that has traditionally attracted many of the brightest minds to America's shores, as well as an unparalleled higher education system. With only 5 percent of the world's population, the United

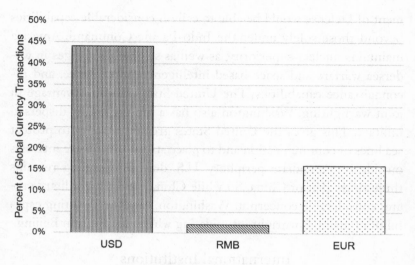

Foreign exchange transactions, 2019
Data from Bank for International Settlements

States accounts for 25 percent of global wealth and 35 percent of world innovation. It is home to nearly 600 of the world's 2,000 most profitable companies, and 50 of the top 100 universities globally.[33] With its strong property rights, flexible labor laws, and dominant multinational companies, the United States traditionally acts like a sponge, soaking up innovations and innovators from around the world. In the annual Global Innovation Index conducted by the World Intellectual Property Organization, the United States came in third—behind only Sweden and Switzerland—while China ranked fourteenth.[34]

The United States' innovative power extends to financial markets. The United States maintains the world's largest reserve currency, accounting for 44 percent of global foreign exchange transactions, followed by the euro with 16 percent of currency swaps, and trailed considerably by the Chinese yuan with only 2 percent of cleared transactions.[35] Capital markets, ranging from venture capital firms to best-in-class asset managers and global banks, allocate resources efficiently within the American economy to spur innovations and create jobs. Having the deepest and most liquid capital markets in the world also enhances the reach and punch of America's economic statecraft.

Economic Weight

Even as China's economy has grown, America's share of the global economy has not shrunk appreciably. According to IMF data, in 1992—at the height of America's post–Cold War dominance in the international system—the U.S. economy accounted for roughly 25 percent of global GDP in nominal terms. In 2017 the United States still accounted for 25 percent. But Europe's and Japan's shares declined (from 13 and 32 percent, respectively), while China's rose (from 2 to 16 percent). China's rise has not come at the expense of America's share of global GDP. Additionally, the gap in overall size

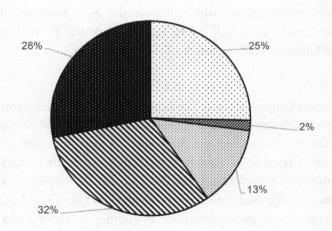

Global shares of GDP, 1990
Data from International Monetary Fund

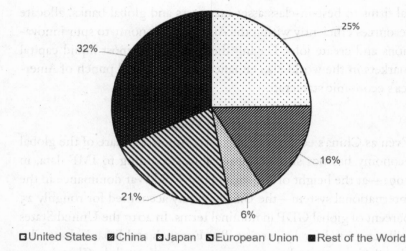

Global shares of GDP, 2019
Data from International Monetary Fund

of both countries' economies in nominal terms has remained relatively steady, with U.S. GDP remaining about $7 trillion larger than China's GDP for much of the past decade.

Energy and Food Security

Whereas China is resource insecure, the United States is the world's largest producer of oil and natural gas. The United States surpassed Russia in 2011 to become the world's largest producer of natural gas and passed Saudi Arabia in 2018 to become the world's largest producer of petroleum. Over the past decade, largely as a consequence of the shale oil and gas revolution, the United States has become an energy superpower.[36] In addition to serving as a significant stimulus to the American economy and a source of innovation within it, the shale energy revolution has also given the United States greater ability to buffer against shocks arising from instability in the Middle East, a condition that China does not enjoy, given its dependence on oil imports from the Persian Gulf.

The United States also has a food security buffer, with abundant arable land and an efficient agricultural sector. These assets enable it to serve as a major exporter, particularly in meats and soybeans, products with significant growth potential as Asian consumers become more affluent and adopt higher-protein diets.

Governance

America's greatest strength is largely intangible. Even during periods of dysfunction, America's political system provides it a distinct advantage over China. The government enforces laws and delivers services, and it is constrained by an independent judiciary and active media that ensure government acts in the interest of the public good. It is a government of the people, by the people, and for the people. The predictable cycles of electoral transitions serve as built-in self-correcting mechanisms whenever policy decisions veer off track and produce poor results. And even when the federal government proves dysfunctional, as it stubbornly has in recent decades and most vividly in its initial response to the COVID-19 outbreak, state and local governments across the country have demonstrated responsiveness to local requirements, helping to support—and not suppress—the ingrained dynamism of American society.

As Michael Green, a Georgetown University professor and former U.S. official, has observed, "The American constitutional system of government creates enormous strengths for the United States in the international system: legitimizing government at home and abroad; regenerating national dynamism; attracting foreign talent and admiration; and binding other powers through the reassuring transparency and accessibility of our political process."[37] China, by contrast, enjoys none of these attributes. It is governed by a small group of individuals committed to preserving power and dependent on security services to protect their privileged position within a rapidly changing society. That is why, as then–vice president Joe Biden used to quip privately to me and others, he would rather have America's challenges than China's any day of the year.

Conclusion

The United States is still—and will long remain—the dominant power in the bilateral relationship. It retains abundant capacity to protect its vital interests while coexisting with an increasingly powerful China. The United States need not—and should not—turn China into an adversary. By the same token, China needs to do more to reassure the United States that it is committed to pursuing a productive relationship, including by not seeking to push the United States out of its role in Asian or global affairs, and by tempering its own actions that are inflaming tensions with the United States.

For the United States, competing with China is mostly about itself—sustaining American advantages, investing in future competitiveness, and strengthening international attraction for principles and values at the heart of the American experiment. This does not absolve the United States from the need for an effective strategy on China, but it does place emphasis where it should be: on improving America's own sources of competitiveness.

In recent years, the United States has been squandering its sources of strength: a strong global network of alliances, international prestige, and national purpose in addressing America's own shortcomings. By inconsistently standing up for democratic values and individual liberties, frequently showing sympathy for autocratic behavior abroad, picking fights with erstwhile allies, fumbling its responses to domestic and international crises, and deepening social divisions at home, the United States has been undermining its own advantages in its competition with China.

The United States' most urgent priority is to right its own course.

America's future will be better served by concentrating on strengthening itself than by seeking to slow down China. And China's future will be better served by avoiding actions that invite great power hostility or conflict.

Both countries require avoiding military conflict to achieve their national ambitions. Neither country can achieve its goals in an outright hostile relationship. Neither country is capable of imposing its will on the other at an acceptable cost or risk. And given the dense webs of interdependence that bind the people of both countries together, it is difficult to envision a scenario whereby one country succeeds while the other fails. They both likely will rise or fall in tandem.

In short, both sides need to invest in making the relationship work. A critical first step in that process is reaching an accurate understanding of the ambitions of the other.

TWO

China's Strategic Ambitions

In this chapter, I examine China's strategic ambitions and where they intersect with America's vital interests. The United States and China have a strong incentive to avoid direct conflict with each other, given the catastrophic consequences that would result from such a collision. Given this dynamic, America's ability to coexist with a powerful China will be strengthened if the United States can help China realize the boundaries of where it can pursue a greater role for itself without coming into conflict with vital American interests, and where it cannot. Doing so will require Washington to be forthright in registering its concerns with Beijing about problematic behavior while remaining able to discriminate between Chinese actions that implicate America's vital interests and those that do not. The United States will have limited influence on China's decisions if it makes every Chinese action everywhere in the world a cause of concern.

Setting the Context
China's rapid ascent in national power has set off a feverish debate in the United States about the scope of Beijing's ambitions. A wave

of books has been published examining China's geopolitical goals and the related question of whether China's ambitions have increased under Xi Jinping's leadership. One of the most prominent—and provocative—of these books is Michael Pillsbury's *The Hundred-Year Marathon*. In it, Pillsbury purports to reveal a secret long-term design by China to overtake the United States and become the world's leading power by 2049. Although prominent China scholars such as Harvard University's Alastair Iain Johnston have exposed the shaky assumptions and flimsy methodology on which Pillsbury's conclusions were based,[1] the argument has nevertheless gained notoriety, so much so that its conclusions have been echoed in Trump administration documents and speeches.[2]

If analyses of China's ambitions were plotted on a spectrum chart, Pillsbury's argument would occupy a space near the outer edge of the alarmist pole. Even observers who do not subscribe to Pillsbury's views, though, are worried about the implications of an ascendant China for America's global standing.[3] These concerns are informed by a near-axiomatic belief that as great powers rise, their ambitions expand. So, the argument goes, even if Beijing does not harbor visions of dominating other regions or displacing the United States from its global leadership role now, it may well do so as it grows stronger. Such concerns are also colored by a judgment, shared by scholars with diverse political leanings, that the United States will not be successful in integrating China into the existing post–World War II international order of institutions, norms, and rules. As the China expert Tom Christensen has written, many international relations scholars "believe that a rising China, especially an authoritarian one, will want to rewrite the rules of the current international order, not accommodate itself" to rules that were established by the United States and others.[4]

My evaluation of China's ambitions has been informed both by scholarly and theoretical writing and by firsthand experiences listening to China's leaders discuss their country's objectives. I first began examining this question as a diplomat in Embassy Beijing from 2009 to 2012, where my primary responsibility was to engage with government officials, advisors, and outside experts and, based on those exchanges, draft a series of classified reports about China's evolving views of its role in the world. From 2013 to 2017, I served as President Obama's National Security Council director for China, Taiwan, and Mongolia. This position provided me an opportunity to interact daily with the best analysts of Chinese statecraft inside and outside the U.S. government. It also allowed me to accompany the president, the national security advisor, and other senior officials in their meetings with members of the Chinese leadership. I sat at the seam of policy and politics, observing how each interacted with the other.

Over years of close observation, I watched Chinese leaders grapple with challenges at home and abroad. I studied their responses to U.S. pressure, and their skepticism about U.S. gestures of strategic reassurance. And I listened closely to the cadence of their complaints that the United States was standing in the way of their national ambitions.

Based on these experiences, I strongly believe that China's leaders have long aspired to restore their country to its self-perceived historical position as the leading power in Asia and a central actor on the world stage. However, the pace and manner by which they pursue these objectives have been—and will be—influenced by circumstances at home and the strategic environment abroad. China has demonstrated itself to be opportunistic in taking steps toward its goals, but not reckless in courting confrontation with the United States in doing so. Beijing views the United States as the most critical external variable in its calculus of how far and how fast to push its agenda. The United States remains the only external actor that could prevent China from realizing its ambitions. When Beijing has bumped up against the prospect of conflict, such as in mooted plans to build an artificial island on Scarborough Shoal in 2016—an action that could have implicated U.S. alliance commitments to the Philippines—it has pulled back.

China's leaders recognize that a strategy of direct confrontation with the United States and its allies would be dangerous and expensive. To be sure, there are advocates within China for advancing down a more militarized pathway for realizing national ambitions, but up to this point, their views have not often prevailed in internal policy debates.

Few in the United States today are comforted by Chinese strategic restraint, though. The picture of where China is seizing initiative and taking actions to advance its interests abroad is much clearer than the picture of where China has pulled back to avoid confrontation with the United States.

How Did We Get Here?

China's pursuit of a larger role for itself in the world has coincided with America's pursuit of a smaller one. At the same time as China has been setting up new multilateral institutions and launching ambitious infrastructure projects to link China to the rest of the world, the United States has withdrawn from the Trans-Pacific Partnership, the Paris climate accord, the P5+1 nuclear accord with Iran, the United Nations Human Rights Council, and the Intermediate-Range Nuclear Forces Treaty, to name but a few examples.

This dual dynamic of Beijing surging forward while Washington steps back has magnified concerns in the United States that China is becoming increasingly assertive and revisionist.[5] Many analysts have associated China's growing ambitions with Xi Jinping.[6] According to this argument, Xi has removed the mask China once used to conceal its ambitions.

China's own narrative of its rise, and of its historical identity, stands in contrast. Many influential Chinese thinkers view China's rise as leading to a restoration of the natural state of international relations, with the country resuming its position as the world's largest economy and leading global actor. China views its "century of humiliation" beginning with its loss to Western powers in the Opium War (1840–1842) and its subsequent political subjugation and national fragmentation as a historical aberration, a stain on the country's long and proud history and a wrong in need of righting.[7]

Under former paramount leader Deng Xiaoping, China adopted a foreign policy strategy of "hiding strengths, biding time, never taking the lead."[8] This strategy served several purposes, for example avoiding great power competition for global influence, evading the burden of global leadership responsibility for addressing problems outside China's borders, reducing risk of encirclement by China's neighbors to challenge Beijing's rise, and enabling China to concentrate resources on its own development.

Before Xi's ascent to the presidency, grumblings had already begun inside China about the continuing efficacy of maintaining such a passive approach to foreign affairs.[9] Many of these grumblings first became audible in autumn 2008. This period coincided with the global financial crisis, an event that made an irreparable dent in American prestige within China.[10] It also coincided with Beijing's successful hosting of the 2008 Summer Olympics. The Olympics were more than just a series of athletic competitions; they were a wellspring of national pride, a cathartic metaphor of China's rise.

As a foreign service officer in Beijing during this period, my job was to make sense of the zeitgeist in China. I spent my days talking with officials and government advisors. Those discussions quickly laid bare that many leading thinkers wanted China to unshackle itself from its timidity and begin acting like the rising global power they perceived it to be.

Many of my contacts told me that China would no longer approach its relationship with the United States as a teacher-student relationship, with China accepting America's advice. They told me that the global financial crisis had shown the flaws in America's political and economic models. Above all, the message I received was that China was done deferring its ambitions. China's time was now.

After a period of uncharacteristically visible debate over China's role in the world, particularly given China's censored media, then–state councilor Dai Bingguo shut down discussion. Dai published an authoritative commentary in official Chinese media in December 2010 reaffirming that conditions were not yet ripe for China to take on greater global responsibilities.[11] Dai asserted that China would continue to adhere to Deng Xiaoping's strategy of "hiding strengths, biding time." Several of my more conservative contacts were relieved, while many others frustratedly grumbled to me that the tide of strategic thinking in China was shifting, even if Dai was too cautious to acknowledge it. With the benefit of hindsight, this latter group clearly was right.

Enter Xi Jinping

When Xi Jinping assumed the presidency in 2013, he inherited significant challenges, both real and imagined. China's export- and investment-led economic model was coming under scrutiny as a viable model for delivering healthy growth into the future. Capital flight was intensifying, raising questions about public confidence in the competence of the CCP's rule. Public dissatisfaction with the scale of official corruption was being magnified through social media, a relatively new and untamed information outlet. A rival of Xi's for China's top leadership position was ensnared in a tawdry affair involving corruption and murder, exposing a lack of discipline at the highest echelons of power. Visible power factions within the Communist Party leadership betrayed a lack of unity. Marxism-Leninism seemed to hold diminishing public attraction. And China's external environment was growing more complex, with the United States launching a "pivot to Asia" that enjoyed broad support throughout the region at the same time as the Arab Spring was sweeping across the Middle East and toppling unelected leaders in its wake.

Senior Chinese officials privately expressed anxiety and bewilderment to me that previously entrenched leaders across the Middle East were falling like dominoes, clearly implying worry that such events could spread to China in the future. As the Chinese international relations expert Wang Jisi has observed, "A unique feature of Chinese leaders' understanding of their country's history is their persistent sensitivity to domestic disorder caused by foreign threats. From ancient times, the ruling regime of the day often has been brought down by a combination of internal uprising and external invasion." Indeed, the collapse of the Ming and Qing dynasties, as well as the retreat of the Kuomintang to Taiwan, all coincided with external events that influenced China's domestic developments.[12]

In many respects, China's foreign policy under Xi Jinping is the story of how Beijing responded to its own vulnerabilities by stoking nationalism and pride in China's rapid rise. From the outset, Xi quickly set a bolder and more assertive tone for China's foreign policy. In November 2013, the People's Liberation Army announced an air defense identification zone over contested waters in the East China Sea. In May 2014, a Chinese national oil company placed an oil rig in contested waters with Vietnam in the South China Sea. In taking these steps, and then later adding to them with land reclamation of seven submerged features and rocks in the South China Sea, Xi gave Chinese citizens confidence that he would harness the country's national power to seize the initiative in territorial disputes with weaker neighbors. Just as Mao had established modern China and Deng had helped China get rich, so Xi pledged to make China strong.

As a step down that path, in November 2014 Xi presided over the funeral of Deng's dictum to "hide your strengths, bide your time, never take the lead." Xi used a rare meeting of the central conference on work relating to foreign affairs—only the fourth such meeting since the founding of the PRC—to outline a more activist approach for China's foreign policy.[13] In laying out his vision for China's future foreign policy direction, Xi judged that the United States would not confront China militarily if it became more ambitious in pursuing its goals, and neighboring countries would not risk severing economic ties with China by pushing back against a more central role for Beijing in regional and global affairs. Both judgments represented calculated gambles by Xi. They also provided Washington with incontrovertible evidence that Xi was unlike his predecessors. Xi showed himself to be risk tolerant, comfortable with friction, and aggressive in pursuit of national ambitions.

Since then, China has launched the first large-scale non–Bretton Woods development bank, the Asian Infrastructure Investment Bank, and attracted nearly one hundred other economies to join. Beijing has advanced the most ambitious infrastructure development project of the past century, the Belt and Road Initiative, with projects spanning Asia, Europe, Africa, the Middle East, and the Americas. It has institutionalized the BRICS (Brazil, Russia, India, China, and South Africa) grouping as a counterweight to Western-leaning groupings such as the G7 and established the BRICS headquarters in Shanghai. It has strengthened its position in the South China Sea. And in a demonstration of its expanding military capabilities, China has fielded aircraft carriers, built its first permanent overseas base in Djibouti, and participated in naval exercises with Russia in the Sea of Japan, the Mediterranean, the Baltic, the Persian Gulf, and elsewhere.

Not since the Cold War has a country contested American leadership in multiple regions of the world simultaneously. Beijing has demonstrated that its ambitions are far from being benign or passive. Indeed, China poses arguably the sharpest challenge to America's traditional global leadership and to the existing system of international rules, norms, and institutions that constitute the international order.

Is Beijing Trying to Export a "China Model"?

Instead of seeking to assuage such concerns, though, China's senior officials appeared to lean into them. In June 2017, Fu Ying, then National People's Congress chairwoman of foreign affairs, acknowledged in an editorial that China's new activism had aroused "unfounded suspicion by some, that China's departure from its longstanding passive posture is a sign of it challenging the U.S.-led world order." However, she concluded, China's strength had reached a level whereby it could afford to push for adjustments that better accommodate China's role in the international system.[14]

A month later, in July 2017, China's top foreign affairs official at the time, state councilor Yang Jiechi, wrote an essay on Xi Jinping's thought on diplomacy, in which he reported, "Xi Jinping pointed out in explicit terms that we are closer than ever to the center of the global stage, that we are closer than ever to fulfilling the Chinese dream of national renewal, and that we are more confident and able than ever to realize this goal."[15] Yang noted that China's foreign policy would be guided by the domestic and international situation. China would tack based on events at home and abroad but would not lose sight of its goal of returning China to its perceived rightful place at the center of the world stage.

Several months later, in October 2017, Xi further stoked national pride in his address to the Nineteenth Party Congress, during which he hailed a "new era" for China and declared: "The Chinese nation, which since modern times began had endured so much for so long, has achieved a tremendous transformation: it has stood up, grown rich, and is becoming strong. . . . It [China] offers a new option for other countries and nations who want to speed up their development while preserving their independence. . . . This is an era that will see China move closer to the center of the world stage and making greater contributions to mankind."[16]

To many longtime China watchers, Xi's speech, while triumphal, also embodied a common rhetorical trope used by leaders dating back to Mao: unite the Chinese people and restore China to a place of power on the world stage. To less seasoned observers, though, Xi's speech represented a turning point, smoking-gun evidence of Beijing's ambition to export an authoritarian "China model" abroad—ushering in a new ideological contest akin to the struggle between communism and democracy during the Cold War.

Xi's speech, paired with the Communist Party's abolishment of term limits for the presidency, its statist turn away from economic reform, and its aggressive efforts to stifle dissent and impose social control, including in Xinjiang, contributed to a major pendulum swing in elite sentiment in the United States toward China. To many pundits and policy makers in the United States, China went from being a competitor with which the United States occasionally cooperates to an adversary that the United States must defeat, even if doing so incurs costs for the United States.[17]

Two months after his address to the Party Congress, Xi sought to tamp down the ideological edge that his previous comments had exposed. He told a high-level gathering of foreign leaders in Beijing that "managing our own affairs well is China's biggest contribution to building a community with a shared future for humanity." He went on: "We will not 'import' a foreign model. Nor will we 'export' a China model, nor ask others to 'copy' Chinese methods." Xi's reiteration of China's desire to steer away from ideological competition with the United States reflected the long-standing position of the Chinese leadership, dating back to the onset of reform and opening in the late 1970s.[18] It was too little, too late.

Xi's low-wattage clarification of China's line did little to arrest the mounting momentum within policy-making circles in the United States toward viewing China's ambitions as ideologically inspired, with the goal of advancing a "China model" and ultimately displacing the United States as the global leader. Even if China did not seek to export its governance model, the argument went, its four decades of rapid economic growth had demonstrated that development did not require democracy. Through the example of its own success, as well as its willingness to invest unconditionally in countries with abysmal governance records, China was generating an authoritarian tailwind. And through its export of surveillance and censorship technologies to the highest bidders, as well as its documented efforts to manipulate public discourse and influence elections in Australia, New Zealand, Taiwan, and elsewhere, China appeared to be weakening individual protections and undermining democratic institutions.[19]

In the ensuing months, a wave of reports emerged focusing on the effects of China's rise on America's global leadership position and America's economic competitiveness. Debates splashed across the editorial pages of leading American newspapers over whether the United States and China were igniting a new Cold War. Prominent commentators such as Robert Kagan warned, "The challenge today to democracy is greater than it was during the Cold War."[20] Kagan observed that "authoritarianism may be a stable condition of human existence, more stable than liberalism and democracy. It appeals to core elements of human nature that liberalism does not always satisfy—the desire for order, for strong leadership, and above all, the yearning for the security of family, tribe, and nation."[21]

Amid these debates, though, three fundamental questions attracted much less scrutiny: First, what is China trying to achieve? Second, what factors will influence China's pursuit of its ambitions and determine whether China succeeds? And third, where do China's ambitions challenge American interests, and where do they not?

What Is China Trying to Achieve?

Part of the difficulty of describing China's ultimate national ambitions on the world stage is that no authoritative document or statement reveals an answer, much less a coherent plan for achieving any such desired end state. Over years of conversations with Chinese leaders and the people who advise them, however, I have come to recognize some rather consistent currents of thought.

China's leaders consistently state that they seek to restore China as a great global power economically, technologically, militarily, and politically by midcentury, in effect returning the nation to its self-perceived historical position in the international community. Xi Jinping often invokes this broad concept when he raises China's two centenary goals: to build a moderately prosperous society by the centenary of the founding of the Chinese Communist Party in 2021, and to build China into "a modern socialist country that is prosperous, strong, democratic, culturally advanced, and harmonious" by the centenary of the People's Republic of China in 2049.[22]

Chinese leaders recognize their governance system is not exportable. They do not face a requirement to build Sinocentric political or military blocs organized in opposition to the United States. Attempting to do so would be too alarming to India, Japan, and others, who would actively challenge any such efforts. Rather than seek to carve the world into Cold War–like configurations, Beijing's proximate goal is to strengthen the legitimacy of the Chinese Communist Party and erode what it views as the bias of key values, norms, and preferences toward democracy, individual rights, rule of law, and Western-led standard setting.

Over the longer term, China aims to become wealthy, strong, influential, and respected. In practical terms, this means China wants to escape the middle-income trap through technological innovation; field a military that is capable of securing China's claimed territory and protecting its access to resources and markets; update international rules and norms to serve its interests; and secure international acceptance for its political and economic models.

China's Core Interests

China's top leadership widely accepts that protecting China's "core interests" is a minimum requirement for the Chinese Communist

Party to preserve its legitimacy as the uncontested governing authority of the People's Republic of China.[23] China's core interests are guided by three prongs: sovereignty, security, and development. Then-state councilor Dai Bingguo defined China's core interests publicly in 2010 as, first, China's political stability, namely, the stability of the CCP leadership and of the socialist system; second, sovereign security, territorial integrity, and national unification; and third, China's sustainable economic and social development.[24]

Leveling the Playing Field in Global Governance

China is no longer content to defer to American leadership on questions of international importance. Former National People's Congress chairwoman Fu Ying has given clearest expression to China's desire to be on par with the United States, not subordinate to it, both in my private conversations with her and in her public speaking and writing. In one speech, Fu examined the distinction between the "world order" that the United States claims to lead, and the "international order" that China identifies with. She explained, "The United States regards China as a newly rising power and wants China to accept its leadership and act as a *subordinate partner*. . . . China uses the term 'international order.' What China is referring to is the international institutions within the UN structure, to which China has a sense of belonging as an *equal member*."[25]

China has been adaptive and opportunistic in securing greater leadership in international institutions. At the time of this writing, Chinese citizens now lead four of the fifteen specialized agencies within the United Nations: the Food and Agriculture Organization, the International Civil Aviation Organization, the International Telecommunications Union, and the Industrial Development Organization. This leadership profile gives China disproportionate influence over setting agendas on a wide array of issues in the international system. By contrast, no other country's citizens lead more than one UN specialized agency.

In other parts of the UN system, such as the Human Rights Council, China has exploited America's absence to reorient the institution's focus toward more favorable terrain—respect for state sovereignty and social stability—and away from protections for individual freedoms. China has also sought to mobilize support through old-fashioned diplomacy for its preferred norms in emerging areas, such as support for the idea of "internet sovereignty," whereby states maintain the right to control internet content within their own borders.

As the China expert Evan Feigenbaum has argued, China is also engaging in "portfolio diversification" with respect to multilateral development banks. China continues to participate in and support all major regional and global development institutions, even as it launches its own. "When China has endorsed new structures, such as the New Development Bank and BRICS contingency reserve arrangement, it has simultaneously made sizeable replenishment contributions to the IMF, where it now has nearly three times the voting weight of Canada, about a third more than Britain and France, and only a whisker less than Japan." Similarly, when China launched the Asian Infrastructure Investment Bank, it ensured that the AIIB built partnerships with every other leading multilateral development bank in the world. In so doing, Beijing is giving itself options—and, by extension, leverage—to move the existing multilateral development banks in its preferred directions.[26]

Seeking Great Power Exemptions from Global Rules

Chinese officials believe their growing weight in the international system affords them latitude to self-exempt from international rules when it serves their interests to do so, much as they assert the United States has done in recent decades. Chinese officials for years have complained that the United States adheres to the UN framework when it meets U.S. needs and takes unilateral actions outside the UN framework when it does not. Chinese officials often cite NATO's decision to conduct an air campaign in Kosovo in 1999, and the United States' military intervention in Iraq in 2002, in both cases without UN Security Council authorization. According to the Chinese argument, when the International Tribunal for the Law of the Sea ruled largely against China's claims in the South China Sea in 2016, the United States was unyielding in its insistence that the ruling was final and binding. Washington was unwilling to grant Beijing any "great power exemptions" to the rules.

Revising Asia's Regional Security Order

China also seeks to alter the military balance in Asia so that it is not so tightly hemmed in within the first island chain, a string of islands extending from Japan through Taiwan and the northern edge of the Philippines to shore in Vietnam. China would like to establish greater freedom of action to move Chinese military ships and submarines through strategic straits out to the Pacific, as well as to reduce the intensity of American military operations near China's shores and in its claimed waters and airspace.

Chinese leaders also wish to weaken and ultimately abolish America's alliance structure in Asia. As a prominent Chinese scholar privately explained to me, "China seeks an Asian security order that is not just underpinned by American alliances and targeted at them, but rather a regional security structure that includes China at its core."[27]

China would like to be seen now as a leader in Asia on par with the United States, and eventually as the uncontested central power in the region. As the asymmetry in military capabilities between China and all its neighbors grows, and all of them become ever more dependent on China for their own economic development, China expects countries throughout the region to become more deferential to its interests.

China also intends to harness its expanding capabilities to resolve territorial disputes in its favor. Beijing seeks to create a fait accompli with its neighbors so that they conclude that the cost of conflict with China is prohibitive and therefore that it serves their interests to sue for peace to avoid costly confrontation with Beijing. China's leaders seek to solidify control of contested territorial claims with India, Vietnam, Malaysia, the Philippines, Brunei, and Japan.

The top leadership also remains fixated on Hong Kong and Taiwan. In the case of Hong Kong, China seeks to pull forward the time horizon whereby it exercises effective control over the city. Beijing agreed to allow Hong Kong to exercise a high degree of autonomy until 2047 as a condition of its return from the United Kingdom in 1997. The longer that time has passed since the retrocession, though, the more interested Beijing has become in stamping out Hong Kong's uniqueness, which Beijing fears could inspire citizens on the mainland to demand equal rights to due process, free expression, and media freedoms that Hong Kong citizens have enjoyed.

President Xi has declared that unification of Taiwan is a challenge "that cannot be passed down to future generations." Whether Xi's statement means Beijing has a timeline for unification is a source of ongoing debate within the China-watching community. I believe that Beijing has confidence that time is on its side, it has many tools in its toolbox short of military invasion to compel Taiwan to pull closer to the mainland, and Xi would prefer not to risk direct military conflict with the United States over Taiwan unless it becomes necessary to halt Taiwan independence.[28] That said, Xi's statement suggests at a minimum that Beijing is dissatisfied with the cross-Strait status quo and is seeking to tilt developments toward Beijing's preferred direction going forward.

Safeguarding China's Political and Economic Model

Politically, Beijing has become more brazen in its efforts to normalize autocracy. Chinese diplomats now routinely and publicly seek to discredit what they term "Western democracy" as being in-efficient at allocating benefits and ineffective at addressing societal challenges. Chinese journals and newspapers echo these efforts, carrying pieces arguing that liberal democracy is a Western conceit that is not well suited to the rest of the world.[29]

China has also sought to regularize its governance practices. Chinese firms have sold surveillance systems, including facial rec-ognition and predictive policing technology, to the highest bidders around the world. Chinese authorities have also sought to stifle open debate on China abroad, particularly among the Chinese di-aspora. Beijing has been buying up media outlets around the world in a seeming effort to monopolize press platforms and influence international discourse on China.[30] Chinese security services have also conducted extraordinary renditions of ethnic Chinese overseas who have been accused of challenging CCP authority.[31]

Economically, China is seeking to use the leverage generated by its role as the leading trading partner with most countries in the world to gain acceptance of its model of state-led industrial capi-talism. Through both threats and inducements, Beijing has sought to deter countries from seeking to challenge its statist-mercantilist economic model. It has adopted highly visible punitive economic strategies against countries like Norway, the Philippines, and the Republic of Korea during dustups over various issues in an effort to signal that there are costly consequences for countries that get crosswise with Beijing.[32]

So, in short, China is a highly strategic revisionist power. It mar-ries ambition and capacity in the most formidable challenge the United States has faced in decades. China seeks to revise the distri-bution of power in the international system, the security order in Asia, the role and remit of international institutions, the work of multilateral development banks, the free flow of uncensored infor-mation across borders, and the liberal nature of the existing inter-national order. Beijing believes that it needs changes to the status quo to reach its objectives of preserving the role of the CCP as the ruling authority in China and of becoming wealthy, strong, influential, and respected on the world stage. These are China's aspirations.

What Factors Will Influence Whether China Succeeds?

America's response needs to be informed by an understanding of how likely China is to achieve its ambitions. China's success should not be taken as a foregone conclusion. Beijing confronts a thicket of domestic and external challenges that, if not effectively managed, could trip up its pursuit of its ambitions. Beijing must also reconcile competing imperatives in pursuit of its goals.

For example, China's ambitions to prevail in territorial disputes and on Taiwan exist in tension with its status quo objectives of preserving regional stability and constructive economic relations with other major powers. China will not be able to develop its economy and simultaneously appropriate the rights and interests of other countries. It will have to choose.

Relatedly, China will be challenged to prevent the emergence of regional countries banding together against Beijing as China's military capabilities bump up more frequently against other regional powers. Already in recent years, China has aroused antipathy by threatening military action against Vietnam and India over territorial issues. Chinese and Japanese naval and air platforms have been operating more frequently and in closer proximity to each other in the East China Sea. Chinese military platforms have faced off in the South China Sea with naval vessels from the United States, South Korea, Australia, France, and the United Kingdom.

Already countries have begun coming together in response to Chinese behavior. This has been apparent, for example, in growing coordination among the Quad countries, namely, Australia, India, Japan, and the United States. It has also manifested in the growing frequency of maritime coordination involving Indonesia, Malaysia, Vietnam, and Singapore, and in environmental and economic coordination among countries in the lower Mekong region. The denser the web of relationships that form in Asia, the less space China has to throw its weight around.

Chinese Power Is Not Translating into Influence

China will face obstacles to projecting hard power and marrying it with political and economic influence at a global level. As the Brookings scholar Bruce Jones has argued:

> To develop the most important feature of global power projection, a global blue water navy, China has to overcome the following obstacles: a highly sophisticated American global navy that shows no signs of giving ground; Japan's not inconsiderable naval capacity right off its eastern shore; a further chain of islands from its northeast to its southeast that can hem in its naval power projection; Europe's residual global navy capacity which, while modest, usefully amplifies U.S. capacity; and India's extremely inconvenient geography and growing appetite for power projection in the Indian Ocean.[33]

Few indications suggest that China has—or will soon obtain—the capacity to devise or impose a political or security order in the Asia-Pacific. As India's former national security advisor Shivshankar Menon has observed, "This is a function not just of the balance of power and the presence of the United States, but of its inability to offer a normative framework, and of the nature of its relations with significant countries like India, Japan, Vietnam, Indonesia, Russia, and others."[34] None of these countries seek a subordinate role for themselves in a new Asian regional framework with China at its core.

At a broader level, China's underlying strategic assumption about influencing neighboring states merits scrutiny. China's regional strategy has been predicated on an assumption that as neighboring countries become more economically dependent and militarily inferior to China, they will become more risk intolerant and less likely to challenge China on matters relating to China's "core interests." According to this logic, Taiwan, Vietnam, and North Korea, given their economic dependence and military inferiority, should be deferential to Chinese priorities, but they are not.[35] This highlights a paradox of China's foreign policy. China has strengthened its capacity to compel countries not to do things—for example, host the Dalai Lama or recognize Taiwan—but it has had much less success at persuading countries to do things that advance China's interests, with the notable exception of Cambodia, which has become a reliable surrogate for China in consensus-based decisions by the Association of Southeast Asian Nations (ASEAN).[36]

One explanation for this apparent Chinese shortcoming in being able to persuade other countries to act on its agenda is its limited attraction. China's tight censorship, shrinking space for civil society, and suffocating efforts at social control—especially in ethnic regions such as Tibet and Xinjiang—do not inspire other countries to draw closer to Beijing. China's naked ambition to sit atop a hierarchical order in Asia also challenges the identities of countries along China's periphery, almost all of which jealously guard their ability to pursue their own interests, as they define them. China's slowing economic growth and mounting domestic challenges will likely dim the appeal of China's governance model in the future. Such an absence of attraction presents a major obstacle to Beijing's gaining consent from other states and publics for China to exercise greater regional leadership.

Belt and Road Initiative: Asset or Liability?

China also faces a challenge in executing the BRI at a level reflecting the outsize expectations it has built for the initiative around the world. Many of the envisioned projects are in regions prone to sectarian violence and political upheaval. The initiative faces many complicated legal obstacles, given the patchwork of national laws that the routes must navigate. Many routes traverse countries with entrenched corruption. Public blowback against China is another risk, particularly if the projects come to be seen as lining the pockets of the powerful, failing to create local jobs, destroying the environment, or being exploitative in nature. Questions have also arisen about debt sustainability for the projects, leading many opposition political parties around the world to grow wary of the initiative out of concern that they will inherit an unpayable debt after they return to power. Such concerns about debt loads will only grow in the coming months and years as many BRI recipients struggle under the weight of COVID-19-induced recessions. For these reasons and more, veterans of the World Bank with deep expertise in infrastructure development have forecast that the Chinese are buying themselves future trouble, and the BRI could become more of a strategic liability than an asset to China over time.[37] If the BRI develops a reputation for overpromising and underdelivering, or worse, it could harm China's international image, causing countries to reassess the risks and benefits of complying with China's requests.

Economic Headwinds

How much runway China has left on its national rise before demographic and economic laws of gravity set in also remains an outstanding question. China is attempting to accomplish what no other country has ever pulled off in its transition from an investment- and export-led growth model to a consumption-based model, all while maintaining high levels of debt as it navigates through the middle-income trap.[38] China's society is also aging rapidly. By 2040, the country's demographic profile could resemble Japan's today, but on a significantly larger and more costly scale. Additionally, as China's citizens become more connected through social media, their ability to organize and mobilize (for example, to demand improvements to water quality or access to education) will grow stronger. The demands of an increasingly educated, wired, urban, and aging citizenry will present a complex governance challenge for the Chinese Communist Party.

Given the scale of the challenges China confronts, it would be a mistake for the United States to assume that Beijing will sail past every obstacle and achieve all its ambitions. Not even Beijing assumes that will be the case. By the same token, it would be irresponsible to base policies on assumptions of Chinese failure. China's economy is likely to cool considerably in the coming years but is unlikely to collapse. The more China's economy cools, the less likely it is that resources will continue to be as readily available for ambitious overseas initiatives as they have been in recent years.

The Intersection of China's Revisionism and American Interests

To navigate the growing challenges posed by China's demands for adjustments to the regional and international order, American policy makers will need to discern where Chinese actions do—and do not—implicate vital national interests. If the United States adopts an all-stick-no-carrot approach and reacts strongly to every instance of China attempting to become more active abroad, the United States will devalue the strength of its warnings. As Henry Kissinger has warned, "A policy that is perceived as having designated China as the enemy primarily because its economy is growing and its ideology is distasteful would end up isolating the United States."[39]

Any American attempt to restrain China's rise would succeed only in converting China from a competitor to an enemy. The United States need not—and should not—go down this path, because the United States still holds the power position in the relationship, and China's future is far from certain. A policy objective should therefore be to steer China's rise toward a trajectory that the United States can tolerate. It is in America's interests to encourage China to be ambitious without becoming aggressive, against either the United States or its allies and security partners.

The United States should be prepared, for example, to welcome China taking on a greater leadership role in rallying others to reduce emissions and raise ambitions for addressing climate change. Washington should support the development of China's humanitarian assistance and disaster relief capacity, including information sharing, joint training, and exchange of best practices. Particularly after the spread of COVID-19 from China, Washington should urge Beijing to prioritize efforts to strengthen domestic defenses against pandemic disease while also contributing more to improving global public health capacity. The world would be a better place if China took further steps to strengthen global disease surveillance monitoring and rapid response capacity to outbreaks, for example. The United States should encourage China to play a more active role in reconstructing war-torn areas in Syria, Iraq, Libya, Afghanistan, and Yemen. It should support the Asian Infrastructure Investment Bank, including by joining it. It should find ways to partner with China to meet the global infrastructure shortfall, including through projects funded by the Belt and Road Initiative. And it should explore opportunities to work with China and others to develop rules and norms in currently ungoverned and undergoverned areas, such as cyber, outer space, autonomous systems, and artificial intelligence.

American "Redlines"

At the same time, the United States should also make clear consistently and at authoritative levels that it has enduring interests where it will be unwilling to yield, and where Chinese probing will invite strong and sharp pushback. These interests include preventing any power from dominating Asia and establishing a closed sphere of influence; maintaining unimpeded freedom of navigation and overflight in accordance with international law; upholding the global credibility of American alliance commitments; preventing efforts to use covert, coercive, or corrupt means to control discourse outside one's borders; and preserving an open, rules-based international trading system. The more clarity Beijing has regarding the strength of America's conviction to uphold these long-standing interests, the less likely China will be to take actions that could court conflict by challenging them.

Conclusion

Now and in the foreseeable future, the United States and China will be the two most powerful actors on the world stage. The gap between these two leviathans and every other country in the world is widening as both countries disproportionately benefit from abundant capital, talent, and clustering effects around technological innovation. Both countries have truly global diplomatic and economic reach. The United States also has global military capacity, and China is likewise rapidly developing its own expeditionary capability.

The United States needs to learn to coexist with a powerful China. At the same time, the United States needs to help China realize the boundaries of where it can pursue a greater role for itself without coming into conflict with vital American interests and values, and where it cannot.

Given the scale of both countries' national ambitions and the strains between them, irreconcilable tensions will generate competition. While ideological tensions between the United States and China certainly remain, we need not see a revival of a Cold War–like universalistic struggle between competing blocs. Instead, both sides should accept the intrinsically competitive nature of their relations, trusting that the side with the best ideas and most compelling record of success will garner the greatest influence in the international system over time.

To borrow an analogy from the Columbia University China scholar Tom Christensen, there are two types of competition between major powers. The first is akin to football, where contact is rough and the objective is to prevent the other side's advance. The second is akin to a running race, where the goal is to outpace the other side.

For much of the past forty years, the United States and China have been engaged in a footrace, where the United States has maintained a sizable lead. In recent decades, though, China has steadily been accelerating its pace and narrowing the gap. In recent years, the relationship has evolved toward a football goal line stand, where progress by one side has been measured as a loss for the other, and where the United States has acted as if its back is up against the goal line and it cannot afford to give an inch.

In the next chapter, I lay out why it would be wise to return the relationship to the analogy of a footrace, and how the United States can sustain its lead in doing so.

THREE

Competitive Interdependence

In this chapter, I develop the concept of *competitive interdependence* as a new framework for understanding the nature of relations between the United States and China. This framework is premised on a judgment that competition will remain the defining attribute of the relationship, and interdependence will be inescapable, given the dense web of financial, trade, scientific, academic, and people-to-people links that bind both countries together. The thick webs that bind them make it virtually impossible for one to inflict harm on the other without hurting itself in the process. Ultimately, though, the principal factor that will determine whether the United States remains capable of preserving a favorable balance of power in the face of China's rise will be the United States itself. The more the United States lives up to its own traditions and values, the better it will be able to protect its interests.

Context

America's relationship with China in recent years has become a topic of national debate. Questions that previously were the principal domain of diplomats and policy makers now are features of Americans' everyday conversations and sources of political debates. What type of relationship with China should the United States pursue? What are America's goals with China? What is the most effective way to achieve them? These questions now touch virtually every American in some form or fashion.

It was not always this way. When Richard Nixon made his historic trip to China in 1972, the country was mired in the Cultural Revolution, one of the most cataclysmically destructive social experiments of the twentieth century. The Vietnam War was raging next door. The scars of the Korean War were still fresh. There was virtually no U.S.-China trade or many expectations of future Chinese economic dynamism.

Few Americans' lives were directly affected by events inside China. The country was seen as a potential strategic asset in the Cold War contest against the Soviet Union. Hard-nosed realpolitik calculations drove the first tentative steps toward a thaw in relations.

For the most part, the original bet paid off. China's warming ties with the United States prompted Moscow to reappraise the threats it confronted, ultimately diverting Soviet national focus and military capabilities from the European theater to regions facing China. China's opposition to Soviet expansionism in the last two decades of the Cold War contributed materially to the success of the containment strategy, leading eventually to the collapse of the Soviet Union.[1]

U.S.-Chinese rapprochement also contributed to a long peace in Asia. After enduring three wars in the preceding four decades that cost the lives of hundreds of thousands of American soldiers, Asia has not undergone a major conflict since the United States and China normalized relations.[2]

China has become a critical source of revenue for many of America's leading firms. It has been the fastest-growing market for U.S. exports for much of the past decade. U.S. firms now generate roughly

$450 billion in revenue by producing in China to sell to the Chinese market, in addition to the $120 billion generated by U.S. exports to China. S&P 500 firms now derive between one-third and one-half of their profits from China.

Progress was also achieved in areas ranging from nonproliferation to climate change, pandemic disease prevention, wildlife protection, and development assistance. As laudable as this progress has been, though, it is not what most animates the views of many Americans on China.

Polling by the Pew Research Center shows that Americans are most concerned about China skirting rules, stealing jobs, and using cyberespionage to pilfer America's trade secrets. For many in the United States, issues of fairness are at the heart of their frustrations with China.[3] And as China's economy increasingly challenges America's as the world's largest and most innovative, Americans' tolerance for Chinese "cheating" appears to be diminishing. Anger about China's initial efforts to cover up the COVID-19 virus outbreak in Wuhan has been overlaid on these long-standing problems, further fueling American resentments toward China.

The Chinese government has brought much of the criticism on itself, through the opacity of its governance system and its stubborn disregard of international urging to abide by market economy principles, among other reasons. Problems arising from China's industrial policies, market access restrictions, technology transfer requirements as a condition of market entry, subsidization of state-owned enterprises, over-capacity production in key sectors, and lax enforcement of intellectual property protections have become too big for the United States or others to overlook. China's naked efforts to privilege national champions over international competitors have generated public resentments that President Trump has seized on to drive American policy toward China in a new direction.[4]

At the same time, the American public's perception of threat from China has not risen to a level that would lead them to accept significant sacrifice in service of confrontation with China. For example, American citizens rank China very low—eleventh, to be precise—in a listing of threats confronting the United States.[5] Another poll by the Pew Research Center asked Americans to rank seven threats, ranging from Iran to North Korea to climate change and terrorist threats. China came in fourth.[6] For most Americans, China simply is not a central preoccupation or type of threat that requires mass mobilization to counter, even if it is an object of growing dissatisfaction.

Surveying American Arguments on China Strategy

For some American observers, the answer to this conundrum of disenchantment with past policy yet unwillingness to accept pain in support of a more confrontational approach has been to seek to darken public perceptions of China in the United States. Such efforts rest on the logic that American people will become willing to make sacrifices if they come to see China as a scary threat. On the extreme end of the spectrum in support of such an approach lies the political operative Steve Bannon. He has taken a leading role in reconstituting the Committee on the Present Danger, a Cold War–era grouping of prominent retired officials and experts whose mission is to mobilize public support for confronting America's existential enemy. The Soviet Union and terrorists have claimed this mantle in the past. Now it rests with China.

Although far less extreme, prominent members of the American expert community on China have similarly been seeking to raise awareness of the threat they perceive from China. Well-known commentators such as Elizabeth Economy, Aaron Friedberg, Orville Schell, and John Pomfret have been declaring in media appearances, speeches, private briefings, and congressional testimony that China seeks to undermine and weaken the United States to clear its own path to global dominance.[7] The political scientists Henry Farrell and Abraham L. Newman have developed a concept of "weaponized interdependence" to describe how a great power like the United States could leverage global networks of informational and financial exchange to gain strategic advantage over other powers such as China.[8] Other members of the U.S. expert community such as Robert Blackwill argue that successive presidential administrations before Trump did not grasp the nature of the China threat, and as a consequence, China rose at America's expense.[9] They believe that China will not change as long as the Chinese Communist Party preserves power. They see China seeking to export its governance model, its statist economic model, and its repressive system of social control. From their perspective, the United States must stand in China's path, even if doing so comes at a material cost.

This view holds significant sway in many parts of the Trump administration's national security establishment below the presidential level, as well as with progressives within the Democratic Party. Proponents of this argument believe that Washington would be wisest to confront China now, while the United States still retains a comparative advantage in national power, rather than fight China later, when China will be stronger. While the specific objectives of such an approach remain fuzzy, the basic assumption is that the United States and China hold irreconcilable national ambitions. China stands too distant from American values to be influenced by diplomacy. Therefore the United States needs to slow down China's rise now to limit Beijing's ability to spread its authoritarian influence and eventually usurp American global leadership. Halting China's progress is the goal, even if it comes at a cost to the United States.

Washington's desire to impede China's path has fed an impulse toward action. At times, action has been confused for achievement. Under the banner of "strategic competition," Washington has sought in recent years to confront Beijing wherever China is perceived to be seeking to expand its influence, with little regard for whether the

Chinese action in question implicates vital American interests. In recent years, national security advisors, secretaries of state, and other prominent advisors to President Trump have made it standard operating procedure to warn audiences from Africa to Europe, the Middle East, and Latin America to be vigilant against China's exploitative ways.[10] In addition to coming across as condescending, such warnings have also fed a perception that the United States now views countries as pawns in a great power competition with China, rather than as partners bound by a shared agenda.

America's global campaign to drum up anxieties about China has contributed to more negative public attitudes toward China in certain parts of the world, although the extent to which this outcome owes to American warnings is debatable.[11] Yet even increasingly negative public perceptions of China have not led any country to align with the United States to contain China or choke its economic growth. Not even the United States' most stalwart friends, such as Japan, Taiwan, and Australia, have shown openness to working with the United States to undermine China's political or economic models. And while the European Union has grown more attentive to risks posed by China's rise, much of the EU's policy remains focused on China's predatory economic actions that challenge European firms, rather than any broad-gauge conception of multidomain strategic competition. Reflecting the more nuanced view of China from Brussels, official EU policy refers to China as a partner, competitor, and systemic rival.[12]

Such reticence from allies to partner with the United States in adopting a policy of unvarnished rivalry stems from the fact that these nations see their economic relationship with China as essential, even as they continue to value their relationship with the United States. As such, Washington's recent bout of enthusiasm for viewing the world through the lens of great power competition has been a uniquely American phenomenon. Consequently, any American attempts to replicate with China America's Cold War experience of containing the Soviet Union would generate more isolation than influence for the United States on the world stage.

Recognizing the limitations of expansive efforts to confront China, a group of realist foreign policy scholars have sensed an opportunity to advocate a more modest goal: keeping problems presented by China away from American shores. This group advocates a strategy of offshore balancing, meaning the United States should withdraw its forward-deployed forces, bring them home, and only intervene militarily if another major power is poised to conquer and dominate a region of strategic significance to the United States. As the University of Chicago's John Mearsheimer and Harvard University's Stephen Walt have written: "The aim is to remain offshore as long as possible, while recognizing that it is sometimes necessary to come onshore. If that happens, however, the United States should make its allies do as much of the heavy lifting as possible and remove its own forces as soon as it can."[13]

Other realists argue that the United States should disentangle itself from alliances, stop pressing to open markets, mute its advocacy of universal values abroad, and retreat behind its oceanic borders and its nuclear umbrella. The case for this isolationist approach was made most famously by the MIT professor Barry Posen in *Restraint*. Posen's argument has gained notoriety in the era of President Trump's "America First" agenda, which at its core argues that the United States should look out for itself and stop trying to solve other nations' problems.[14]

The limits of these arguments for using the Pacific and Atlantic Oceans as buffers against foreign threats have been exposed by the reality that many of the most pressing transnational threats of the twenty-first century are indifferent to borders or geographical buffers. COVID-19 has provided a devastating reminder of the limits of retrenchment. Even if the United States retreats behind its borders, it will still remain vulnerable to diseases, financial crises, cyberattacks, climate change, and other twenty-first-century transnational challenges.

Other experts have been advocating for accommodating China's rise rather than contesting it. Scholars such as Hugh White and Lyle Goldstein have urged the United States to avoid having to choose between withdrawing from Asia and waging war against China to preserve a privileged position there. To avoid such an outcome, White proposes an exchange: the United States would not contest efforts by China to establish much greater influence in its neighborhood, and China would agree to honor vital American interests, such as the maintenance of alliances and the continued presence of U.S. forces in the western Pacific. White encourages the United States to seek a concert of powers in Asia, where the United States would maintain a presence, but China would establish a more leading role for itself.[15]

Whether the argument is for offshore balancing or isolationism or accommodation, the pitfalls share similar traits. They would all impale the credibility of America's alliance commitments worldwide, thereby damaging one of America's greatest comparative advantages. Moreover, history has shown that ceding hierarchical spheres of influence to rising powers intensifies competition and makes conflict more likely, as major powers test boundaries to define the outer edge of where they are able to establish dominance. Strategic imperatives often overtake market principles in determining trade and investment flows, thus leading to worsening economic performance. American allies would hedge against American unreliability by strengthening relations with China, leaving the United States with diminished influence in the region that will serve as the engine of global economic growth in coming decades. Put simply, retreating from a leadership role in the Pacific would invite more danger and less prosperity for the American people.

The Need for a New Approach to China

Fashioning a China strategy in a post-American-primacy world is a formidable challenge. Bill Burns, the most accomplished American diplomat of his generation, has observed:

> Neither unthinking retrenchment nor the muscular reassertion of old convictions will be effective prescriptions in the years ahead. . . . Asia must continue to be our first priority. The most critical test of American statecraft is managing competition with China, cushioning it with bilateral cooperation wherever our interests coincide, and a web of regional alliances and institutions that amplify our leverage. Our economies are deeply intertwined, but that is not in itself a guarantee against conflict. Both the United States and China will have to work to ensure that our inevitable disagreements do not spiral out of control. . . . The primary aim is not to contain China or force others to choose sides, but to ensure that China's rise doesn't come at the expense of everyone else's security and prosperity.[16]

Burns, in my view, has identified the contours of a new strategy toward China well. He believes, as do I, that the United States does not have the option of imposing its will on China any more than it was able to do so in Afghanistan, Iraq, Libya, Syria, or Venezuela. If the United States cannot bend Cuba to its will, then it is unrealistic to expect it will be able to do so with China.

Strategies that assume American muscularity will deliver Chinese concessions or collapse are built on fantasies. They treat the relationship as unidirectional and willfully disregard the myriad ways in which China is capable of imposing strategic and economic pain on the United States. They also ignore Xi Jinping's own domestic politics. Xi has discarded his predecessors' focus on building "harmony" and replaced it with an emphasis on "struggle." In Xi's telling of events, China faces a period of concentrated risks and unprecedented challenges; only a strong Communist Party with a determined leader can steer China through this time of testing. Given this domestic narrative, American strategies that rely on public pressure to produce Chinese capitulation are more likely to compel Xi to counterpunch as a sign of his—and China's—resolve than to elicit compromises on American priorities.

To guard against the emergence of a relationship of outright enmity that would produce no winners and serve neither side's interests, we need a new framework. Such a framework needs to be broad enough to allow both sides to pursue their national ambitions, but concrete enough to give both sides confidence that a competitive yet generally stable relationship is more conducive to mutual security and prosperity than an outright hostile competition for dominance. Dominance is not a viable option for either Washington or Beijing, and accommodation is not an option that either country's political systems would embrace.

Out of necessity, the United States and China will have to find a way to coexist, albeit in an increasingly competitive environment. As two of the leading foreign policy thinkers in the Democratic Party, Kurt Campbell and Jake Sullivan, have written, "Coexistence means accepting competition as a condition to be managed rather than a problem to be solved."[17]

In the present moment, arguments for coexisting with China as a peer competitor may feel like a step backward, given America's multidecade run of unrivaled unipolarity in Asia. The truth, though, is that America's competitive coexistence with other powers in Asia represents a return to the historical norm. Even as the embers of World War II were still flickering, the American strategist George Kennan could already foresee that U.S. primacy in Asia would not be perpetual,[18] and preservation of primacy would not be essential for protecting America's vital interests. Kennan's analysis was informed by America's national experience in Asia before World War II, and it has proved prescient since.

Competitive Interdependence

The United States and China now find themselves locked into a state of competitive interdependence. This original framework, which I seek to advance in this book, is built on a recognition that China simultaneously is America's most formidable multidomain competitor and its most capable potential partner in confronting common transnational challenges. I foresee very few scenarios whereby one succeeds while the other falters.

From an economic standpoint, the tightness of the interdependence created by as much as $600 billion in annual bilateral trade, plus the $450 billion in sales by U.S. firms in China to the Chinese market, constrains options for coercive cost imposition in either direction. The tit-for-tat unilateral tariffs by the United States and China under Trump and Xi have explored the boundaries of cost imposition, demonstrating that both sides are capable of hurting

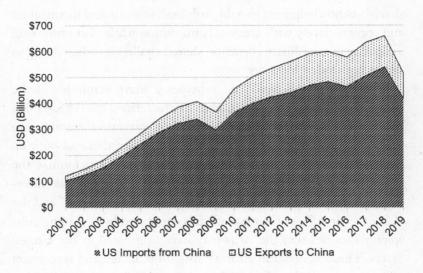

Total U.S. trade with China, 2001–2019
Data from U.S. Census Bureau

each other, but not necessarily of causing the other to accede to demands over how economies and societies should be organized.

From a strategic standpoint, as global actors, both countries increasingly share exposure to risk of instability in every corner of the world. Both are negatively affected by the spread of pandemic diseases, drug flows from Central Asia, terrorist threats from the Middle East, Iran's nuclear program, proliferation risks from North Korea, and piracy off the Horn of Africa. Both confront common challenges from global warming, instability induced by refugee flows, oil market disruptions, and interruptions to the global food supply. The inescapable reality, as former U.S. ambassador to China Jon Huntsman has observed, is that American and Chinese futures are linked.[19]

Such interdependence incentivizes avoidance of direct confrontation. Each side must contend with the fact that if it causes the other to fall, it, too, will get hurt in the process. Over time, this shared acknowledgment should push both sides to deal forthrightly and constructively with areas of contestation while also preserving a capacity to coordinate efforts on shared challenges when doing so serves both sides' interests.

The COVID-19 pandemic provides a sharp reminder of the competitive interdependence that characterizes the U.S.-China relationship. At the outset of the crisis, both countries' responses to each other reflected an instinctual confrontation that had built up over previous years. Both sought to denigrate and demonize the other for being the cause of the suffering that the world was enduring. American officials labeled the virus the "Wuhan virus" and the "Chinese virus," and Chinese officials countered by spreading conspiracy theories that the virus may have originated in the United States. These adversarial efforts harmed the image and reputation of both sides and shrank space for any type of bilateral coordination to emerge in containing the spread of the virus.

Global pandemics, by their very nature, threaten citizens in both countries until the virus is eradicated in every corner of the world. The only way that the virus will get stamped out in every corner of the world is if a consortium of powerful countries and institutions mobilizes resources to develop and deliver a vaccine. No country can achieve such an outcome on its own. The only way that a meaningful coalition of powers will come together is if the United States and China, as two of the world's strongest public health powers, stand at the forefront of such efforts.

This crisis has shown the limits of "strategic competition" as an organizing principle for America's approach toward China. The purely competitive framing of the relationship has limited America's ability to enlist China in efforts to address a global pandemic. The COVID-19 crisis has revealed the need for a durable strategy that can carry on through disturbances and crises and can preserve capacity for coordination even amid intensifying competition.

America's Top Objectives

A shared framework would help conceptualize the nature of competition with China, but it would not answer the fundamental question on which strategy is based: what vital interests must Washington protect in its relationship with Beijing, and how best to do so?

To answer this question, one must begin by examining America's top global priorities and then identify how those global priorities guide American objectives in Asia, and then with China. At a global level, the United States has generally maintained three strategic pillars over the past decades, albeit with lesser emphasis under President Trump: first, advance the security of the United States, its citizens, and U.S. allies and partners; second, promote a strong, innovative, and growing U.S. economy within an open international economic system; and third, advance respect for universal values around the world, including promoting democracy, human rights, and rule of law. Underlying these pillars in the post–World War II era has been a determination to remain the uncontested, preeminent power in the international system. By and large, America's foreign and defense policy decisions over decades and through Democratic and Republican administrations have been guided by these consistent objectives.

In Asia, these broad global strategic pillars have manifested in four broadly consistent objectives since the end of World War II: first, prevent the region from becoming a source of direct threats to the U.S. homeland; second, prevent a hostile power from dominating the region and pushing America out; third, ensure the region remains open to American commerce; and fourth, encourage progress toward respect for rule of law, human rights, and political liberalism. These requirements have driven American decisions on maintaining a forward military presence in Asia, including within the first island chain that runs from Japan through Taiwan and the Philippines. American strategic planners have long viewed maintaining a constant presence within the first island chain as necessary to uphold the credibility of America's security commitments to allies and partners, to ensure open and unimpeded economic access, and to check any Chinese ambitions to establishing hegemony over a closed sphere of influence in East Asia. The Trump administration has placed different weighting on separate aspects of these priorities, including elevating its emphasis on sovereignty. The Trump administration has also pursued goals in a different fashion from its predecessors, but it has not abandoned long-standing American objectives in Asia.

Turning to China, the goal of American strategy need not be—and should not be—to seek to defeat or collapse the country, as it was with the Soviet Union during the Cold War. Rather, a central goal is to encourage China to become ambitious without becoming aggressive. In practical terms, this means that the United States should be prepared to accept China's expansion of influence, as long as China's rise is peaceful and noncoercive and within the bounds of international law and norms. On the other hand, if China seeks to assert influence over other parties through threats, coercive economic measures, or use of force, the United States will need to register resistance, though the exact form and intensity of pushback will have to be calibrated to match the degree of American interests that are implicated.

Maintaining this posture in the face of China's rapid growth in national power will be a tough test for the United States and its security partners. It will require them to maintain sufficient strength to deter Beijing from employing coercive tactics to seize contested territory, particularly territories covered by American security commitments to allies and partners. If the United States is seen as tolerating China's coercion of its allies in Asia, then the global value of America's alliance commitments will plummet, thereby eliminating one of America's most valuable sources of strength and influence.

America's top objectives with China are not just defensive. America would also benefit from China opening more of its economy to outside competition and creating a level playing field for foreign firms to compete alongside their Chinese rivals. The United States also has a strong interest in encouraging China to make more and better contributions to tackling global challenges. Inside China, the United States must also press Beijing to strengthen protections for the rule of law and human rights. One can see little hope for a durable relationship that enjoys the support of the American people without progress on this front.

So, in sum, the United States' top objectives with China as part of a competitive interdependence framework are fourfold: first, to deter Beijing from establishing a hierarchical sphere of influence in Asia and to uphold the global credibility of American security commitments; second, to encourage China to assume greater global responsibility for tackling transnational challenges; third, to push China to open up its markets to outside competition; and fourth, to encourage China to become more responsive to the demands of its citizens. A goal of this approach is to channel China's growing power into areas that will not instigate conflict with the United States, and could help reduce the burden on the United States for addressing global challenges.

None of these objectives require the United States to dominate China, compete with China in a zero-sum "king of the hill" pursuit of primacy, or change China's political system. All of them are more within reach if the United States is working in lockstep with allies and partners to push China's rise onto a nonhostile trajectory. The more the United States and its partners can forge consensus around shared priorities on China and then act to further them, the better the odds that the United States will be able to preserve a favorable balance of power that protects space for all countries to pursue their interests as they define them.

Preventing Chinese Hegemony

As Richard Armitage and Joseph Nye wrote in an influential report, the key to a successful China policy is "getting Asia right."[20] Allies and partners must lie at the heart of any American strategy to influence China's rise.[21] For this reason, the United States needs an Asia strategy for dealing with China, rather than a China strategy for Asia. The challenges presented by China (for example, its revisionist ambitions, discussed in chapter 2) simply are too big for the United States to address on its own. And as the Trump administration's paltry record of achievements in influencing Chinese behavior through insults and unilateral pressure has shown, a go-it-alone approach is not a basis for effective strategy.

Under the long shadow that a rising China casts over the region, the Asia-Pacific provides fertile ground for the United States to build strong alliances and partnerships. American allies and partners share a common trait: none of them want to be subordinated within an exclusive Chinese orbit and be forced to commit to Beijing's goals.[22] Most countries seek constructive relations with both Washington and Beijing. Washington needs to help them hedge, rather than forcing them to choose. As long as countries maintain enough autonomy to pursue their interests as they define them, any Chinese ambition to dominate the region will be frustrated.

Countries along China's periphery need to believe they have options other than relying on China for their security and economic growth. This explains why virtually every country in Asia (including the United States) has a broadly shared objective to develop a dense web of relationships between and among countries in the region. Such efforts are advanced through regional institutions, multilateral trade agreements, military exercises, and combined patrols of major waterways, as well as issue-specific groupings, such as combined fisheries patrols in the South China Sea and joint water management projects around the Mekong. The more the region coheres in addressing common challenges, the less space China has to isolate and intimidate countries into bowing to its will.

Washington can take clear steps to nurture a denser web of relationships across the region. These include reorienting the focus of its relationships with partners and allies from security issues toward tackling common challenges. Although the first obligation of alliances and partnerships is to provide for common defense against external threats, security issues need not remain the only priority. America's partnerships across the region can and should become platforms for building regional capacity, promoting inclusive economic development, and strengthening regional resilience, particularly on climate change adaptation, public health preparedness, and human capital development. The United States does not need to confront China militarily, constrain China's growth, or contain it within its borders to guard against Chinese hegemony in Asia. America can protect its interests with a more indirect approach of catalyzing regional integration on the issues that matter most to the people of the region.

Any strategy designed to deny China the ability to dominate Asia must also have a strong military component. Although the primary domain of competition is unlikely to be the battlefield, the contest for leadership in Asia will certainly be informed heavily by both real and perceived calculations of raw power, both now and in the future. For this reason, the United States and its partners must preserve the ability to deter Chinese efforts to threaten or employ force to achieve strategic objectives. In chapter 5, I discuss in greater detail steps that the United States and its security partners could take to strengthen their deterrent capability vis-à-vis China.

Securing More and Better Contributions from China to Global Challenges

At the same time as it invests in efforts to blunt Beijing's ability to achieve objectives through the use or threat of force, the United States will also need to find ways to elicit more and better contributions from China for addressing transnational challenges. Both the United States and China possess a unique capacity to contribute to global progress and prosperity. Their contributions to security and economic development can either be amplified through coordination or undermined by working at cross-purposes.

Three broad lines of effort could support the objective of encouraging China to shoulder a greater share of the burden in tackling common challenges: first, investing in reassurance alongside deterrence and demonstrating interest in finding a durable strategic equilibrium with China in Asia; second, seizing opportunities to coordinate on common challenges; and third, supporting and welcoming a greater role for China on the world stage in every area where greater Chinese activism does not undermine vital American interests.

Strategic Reassurance

Many so-called China hawks in the United States have concluded that efforts at reciprocal reassurance are meaningless because America and China hold antithetical national ambitions and neither side would trust any assurances offered by the other. These critiques have merit, but they miss the bigger picture. The audience for American efforts to reassure China is not just in Beijing but also in capitals of countries with which the United States seeks to partner in Asia and beyond. Attracting support for its vision of the region's future requires the United States to demonstrate that it discards false binary choices between U.S. primacy in Asia and accommodation of Chinese leadership in the region. A steady stream of speeches and commentaries by leaders and leading thinkers throughout Asia demonstrates that the rest of the region does not buy into such simplistic logic.[23]

Instead Washington needs to present itself as the responsible actor in seeking to prevent the emergence of unvarnished great power confrontation in Asia. Visible demonstrations of effort to reassure China of the United States' intentions, and of its willingness to forge a durable strategic equilibrium with China in Asia, will give countries in the region greater confidence in working with the United States without fear of sacrificing their relations with China in the process.

For example, it would come at little cost for the United States to clarify that its strategy focuses fundamentally on preserving a balance of power grounded in common adherence to shared rules that protect space for countries to pursue their interests as they define them. U.S. strategy is not about containing China, nor is it about dictating how Chinese society organizes itself within its own borders. It also is not about carving the Asia-Pacific into pro-American and pro-Chinese camps. The United States does not seek to limit China's economic growth or diplomatic relations with other states. And the United States should dispense with criticism of countries that accept Chinese investment and assistance, as it has done repeatedly during the Trump administration in its effort to dampen demand for China's Belt and Road Initiative. Countries have agency for deciding where and how to engage with China. Those decisions do not belong to the United States.

The United States could also privately propose to acknowledge that it is unrealistic for Washington to determine how China governs itself and expect in return that China will agree not to use coercive, covert, or corrupt means to manipulate public attitudes in the United States or use technological tools to sow disinformation. Given Beijing's fears of losing domestic information dominance over the narratives of its top leaders, and specifically its fears of public exposure of corruption or malfeasance at the top rungs of the Communist Party, China's leaders would have a natural incentive to establish a private understanding with Washington regarding the need for reciprocal restraint around domestically targeted influence operations. By agreeing to treat each other's domestic political systems as out-of-bounds, both sides would be able to concentrate on managing other areas of bilateral competition while preserving capacity to coordinate on shared challenges, such as pandemic prevention and climate change.

If such signals of reassurance are not reciprocated by Beijing, and if Beijing proves unwilling to engage in sustained and authoritative efforts to forge a durable strategic equilibrium that allows both major powers to coexist and compete according to a common set of rules, the region will know the source of the obstruction. This, in turn, will strengthen Washington's ability to attract regional support for its vision of an equitable and inclusive Asia-Pacific.

Coordination on Common Challenges

Just as the United States and China confronted a common threat during the Cold War, so both nations confront myriad shared challenges today (pandemic disease, climate change, nuclear nonproliferation, cross-border cyberattacks, and so on). A persistent, authoritative set of dialogues at the cabinet and subcabinet levels that report to both leaders could help provide greater shared insights into each other's objectives and reveal opportunities for more equitable contributions toward addressing shared challenges.

Three principal reasons exist for the United States to revive direct and sustained dialogue with Chinese authorities. First, both countries face real and proximate threats that neither can address on its own. COVID-19 provides the nearest example, but so too does climate change. If the United States and China are not on the same page, prospects for progress are greatly diminished. Second, the Trump administration's diplomatic record with China demonstrates that the absence of functioning channels of communication below the president disadvantages America's ability to advance its objectives and protect its interests. The Trump administration conducted an experiment of withholding engagement until China accepted American demands, and it largely failed to elicit Chinese concessions on American priorities. Third, visibly engaging Beijing opens up more space for other countries in Asia to work with the United States on regional priorities without concern that doing so could be seen as favoring one major power over the other. When Washington and Beijing are in regular and visible communication, there is less worry in regional capitals that working with Washington could be interpreted as working against Beijing.

In addition to addressing natural areas of international focus, such as COVID-19, global economic recovery, and climate change, both sides would also benefit from exchanging best practices on common domestic challenges. These could include managing the social, environmental, and economic impacts of population shifts to urban centers. With China becoming the world's second-largest medical and pharmaceutical market and both countries confronting aging populations, U.S.-China cooperation on health care could also prove productive. For global development programs, both nations would benefit from expanding coordination to avoid redundancy, developing metrics to assess the effectiveness of aid, and sharing best practices for delivering overseas disaster response assistance. The more capable China is of responding to natural or man-made disasters, the less burden the United States will shoulder.[24]

Another area where the United States and China share common purpose is in mitigating the adverse social impacts of automation, artificial intelligence (AI), and globalized trade. China is facing as many disruptive challenges from what has become known as the "fourth industrial revolution" as the United States, but because of China's censored media and closed political system, the social dislocations often garner less public focus in China than in the United States.

As world leaders in AI, the United States and China each will need to consider how to reform educational systems, cope with widening wealth inequality, preserve social cohesion, update social safety nets, and find productive ways for displaced workers to feel connected to communities. Each will also contend with how to seize opportunities presented by AI to improve the national condition. For example, both countries would benefit by pooling resources and data to discover cures for cancer and other diseases and to identify the most efficient care models for treatable conditions.[25]

Greater Acceptance of a Growing Chinese Role on the World Stage

Shared buy-in for an approach anchored in competitive interdependence would also be enhanced by America accepting a greater role for China on the world stage. Such acceptance need not be born of altruism or goodwill. Adjustments to the international system to better reflect China's growing stature are both reasonable and practical, if one accepts the goal of system preservation and adaptation without war.

To preserve the functionality of the existing American-led international order and keep China inside the tent, the United States will need to acknowledge several inconvenient realities. First, the United States must recognize that it, too, is a revisionist power, constantly seeking adaptations to the existing system to best suit its needs. The United States has been unabashed about bending the system when it has felt a need to defend its interests, even if the action in question is not permitted under existing laws and rules. Cases in point include U.S. interventions in the Balkans, Panama, Haiti, and Iraq (2003) without United Nations Security Council authorization. The United States has also been revisionist in its approach to trade issues, for example by pushing the concept of managed trade between countries and by invoking national security exemptions to justify tariffs, even when doing so runs counter to the spirit, and at times the letter, of World Trade Organization rules.

Second, Washington will need to acknowledge the merits of the Chinese argument that institutions should adapt to reflect current power realities, not the power balances of past decades. Western European countries do not wield the same level of influence in the international system that they did at the end of World War II. Rising powers, like China and India, deserve a larger say in existing institutions, and western European representation will likely need to be revised downward.

Rebalancing the relative weight of rising powers within existing institutions will come with challenges. Broadly speaking, the more "Western" an institution, the more reliably supportive it has been of democratic ideals and universal values. Think of the G7, for example, a grouping of democratic countries that does not include China or Russia. The more that international institutions adapt to reflect current power realities, the more challenging it will be for the United States reliably to get its way within them. This type of trade-off will be needed to preserve the existing system, albeit in updated form.

Third, the United States will need to overcome its reflexive opposition to Chinese foreign policy initiatives. The United States does not get a vote in whether China pursues projects at home and abroad that expand its footprint and increase its influence. If China wants to devote its resources to creating a development bank or building roads and pipelines, the United States should not—and need not—stand in its way. The United States would earn more influence in the international system by supporting a role for China on the world stage commensurate with its growing power and then insisting that China act in a manner that undergirds—and does not undermine—the founding purposes of existing institutions.

The United States can afford to take a magnanimous approach. It has the strongest global network of allies and partners the world has ever known. It has access to globally distributed military basing. It has the world's most lethal fighting force. It sits at the center of many of the world's institutions whose mission is to govern global commons, manage interstate competition, and facilitate fair trade.

Instead of objecting to every Chinese initiative, the United States should push back only in areas where top national security interests are implicated. In concrete terms, the United States should narrowly concentrate on preventing China from settling interstate disputes by force or from closing access to international waters or airspace. The United States should work with allies and partners to develop strategies that create costs that exceed benefits for Chinese "gray-zone strategies" of working below the threshold of military conflict to assert control over contested territory. Washington should work proactively with third countries to limit China's ability to acquire exclusive use of ports along trade routes that could be used to threaten or cut off sea lines of communication. The United States will need to prevent China from seeking to corner the market on raw materials, including energy supplies and inputs into high-technology manufactured goods. Washington will need to build a unified front with other countries and with the private sector to resist attempts by China to use market access as a blunt tool to compel countries and companies to accede to Beijing's demands. The United States will also need to support third countries in strengthening respect for rule of law, human rights, free media, and representative government, not as a challenge to China but as a check against China seeking to push other countries toward emulating its own repressive political model. The United States will also need to build normative support among allies and partners for viewing it as unacceptable for China—or any other country—to seek to use coercive, corrupt, or covert means to manipulate public attitudes abroad.

If China seeks to play a greater role on the world stage in areas outside these narrowly proscribed zones, the United States should be prepared to tolerate, if not welcome, China's contribution. Such an approach will entail trade-offs. It may lead to reduced efficiency and effectiveness in certain instances, as China's involvement either stymies collective action or redirects it in ways that are suboptimal from an American perspective. For example, China will likely use its growing voice within the United Nations system to more brazenly obstruct efforts to censure human rights abuses in other countries, given China's interest in delegitimizing efforts to place pressure on countries for events that occur within its borders.

China's growing centrality in multilateral bodies may push the United States to rely more on creating and leading issue-specific ad hoc groupings to advance its foreign policy priorities. In so doing, Washington could draw from the example of the anti-ISIL coalition, a grouping of countries that coordinated assets and actions to support a shared objective: defeating ISIL in Syria and Iraq. The important point is that the United States needs to find ways to preserve and adapt the existing postwar international order, an order that has generated significant strategic dividends for the United States, rather than seek to defend it from change and, in so doing, risk its demise.

Even if the United States does all these things, though, the U.S.-China relationship will still remain imperiled under the weight of American public dissatisfaction unless two other critical issues also show signs of directional progress. The first is market access for American firms in China, and the second is human rights protections for Chinese citizens. Both issues color how China is viewed inside the United States and, by extension, influence the amount of political space that is available to any U.S. administration to pursue a constructive relationship with China.

Economic Fairness

One way that leaders in the United States and China could impose boundaries on competition and provide direction and predictability to the economic relationship would be to forge a consensus around a set of shared principles. This would signal to markets that both sides will work within accepted parameters to narrow differences over time. For example, both leaders reasonably could agree publicly on the following points:

- Nonreciprocal market access is not sustainable and, left unchecked, will push the relationship in a confrontational direction.
- Both countries should grow trade to shrink the trade deficit, rather than choke trade to collapse the trade imbalance.
- Both countries should move continually in the direction of exposing more of their economies to competition.
- Recognizing that the WTO lacks answers to pressing challenges facing the twenty-first-century global economy, both countries will support efforts to update WTO rules to establish new global disciplines for forced technology transfer, protection of intellectual property, digital trade and data flows, and government subsidies to state-owned enterprises.[26]

Shared acceptance of such a framework would create space for policy makers on both sides of the Pacific to chip away at problems arising from China's industrial policies, restrictions on market access, subsidization of state-owned enterprises, over-capacity production in key sectors, and lax protection of intellectual property, just to name a few prominent examples. It is reasonable to expect

China's economy to become more market oriented over time, not out of deference to American concerns but rather in recognition that China's modernization will be strengthened by greater outside competition.

A framing goal of America's economic policy toward China should be to take steps that create jobs and raise wages for American workers. For any strategy to enjoy broad public support, it will need to give greater attention to the concerns of labor unions, environmental groups, and constituencies that have grown opposed to trade with China.

Without such support, there is risk that pressure will build over time in the direction of economic decoupling, however improbable such an outcome would be for two countries with a $700 billion trade balance. Efforts by either side to decouple the economic relationship would reduce efficiencies, lower growth, and create inflationary pressure as goods and services become more expensive. Both sides would also feel the need to pursue relationships and blocs for the purposes of strengthening each side's ability to challenge the other.

Such unbridled great power competition, paired with rising economic protectionism, would place global growth and stability at risk. It would also bear an uncomfortable resemblance to previous periods of great power rivalry, including the nineteenth-century competition between Germany and Great Britain that ushered in the conditions leading to World War I. If such a sequence were to occur, it would not just be the economic relationship that would suffer a sharp downturn.[27]

Human Rights

At the same time, the United States also needs to find ways to push China to better protect the rights of its citizens. Without progress on this front, little space will exist in the U.S. political context for pursuing constructive relations. To seek to advance the U.S.-China relationship while human rights conditions in China move backward would be to swim against a strong current.

In recent years, China has experienced deteriorating human rights conditions. Space for dissent has shrunk, access to uncensored information has been reduced, many parts of civil society have become stifled, and room for religious observance has been squeezed. At least one million and perhaps more ethnic Uighurs are being "reeducated" in barbed-wire facilities across Xinjiang without due process. Tibet's unique culture is being trampled. Beijing has cultivated a climate of fear with an increasingly sophisticated surveillance state that is burrowing into every corner of society, creating what some now describe as a model of digital authoritarianism.[28] And efforts to erode Hong Kong's unique legal and social systems are triggering massive protests in Hong Kong and generating significant angst in the United States.

At the same time, the United States also cannot be blind to the gap between rhetoric and reality in how it is living out its ideals at home. On issues ranging from race relations to due process for illegal immigrants and equal access to opportunity, the United States is falling short of its professed ideals. America will have to restore the power of its own example to improve its ability to influence outcomes in China.

Change in China will occur on China's timelines, not America's. Even so, the United States would be unwise to overlook the profound concerns many Americans have about human rights conditions inside China. These issues must remain at the center of the bilateral relationship.

It will be critical for American interlocutors (both official and unofficial) to pursue creative ways of urging Chinese authorities to be more responsive to the will of their citizens, even as they also consistently register objections to erosions of human rights conditions inside China. There may be scope for progress on technocratic issues such as food safety, equal access to education, improving air and water quality, rule of law and due process protections, disability rights, and protections for victims of sexual abuse. Progress on these issues would not offset other egregious human rights violations within China, but it would encourage China to do more to unlock the potential of its citizens. It would also show Chinese citizens that the United States is advocating for their interests. The greater the level of goodwill inside China toward the United States, the more pressure the Chinese leadership will feel to address issues of importance in the overall bilateral relationship.

Conclusion

The strategy I have outlined in this chapter is grounded in an acceptance of China's rise, a determination to work with allies and partners to influence China's rise in a manner that is ambitious without becoming aggressive, and a willingness to push back in areas where China's actions directly implicate vital American interests. The strategy is guided by a judgment that it would serve American interests for China to take on a greater share of responsibility for addressing global problems.

Given its abundant advantages compared to China, the United States need not fear China's rise and need not concentrate national resources on seeking to blunt it. A competitive yet generally stable relationship with China is more conducive to American security and prosperity than an outright hostile one.

This strategy also rests on an understanding that Chinese leaders fundamentally respect strength and resolve but will respond disproportionately to any perceived American efforts to humiliate them publicly. As the stronger power in the relationship, Washington would be wise to focus its private communication with Chinese leaders on the limits of its tolerance of Chinese behavior and the vital interests that it is committed to upholding, rather than engaging in public spats or clumsily attempting to drive a wedge between the Communist Party leadership and the Chinese people.

Some may argue that this approach resembles efforts under previous administrations, including the Obama administration in which I served. Many American experts believe China became a more dangerous threat to the United States during the period when President Obama pursued a balanced approach of seeking to maximize cooperation and manage competition with China. Those experts often criticize the Obama administration's record as failing to deter China's external ambitions and mellow its internal repression.

The approach I have outlined diverges from past approaches in several key areas. First, it provides a narrower identification of areas where the United States should push back against Chinese activism, and calls for more forceful responses in instances when Chinese actions implicate vital American interests. It places a higher priority on rallying like-minded countries, not to challenge China but to support an affirmative vision for the region. It concentrates on denying China strategic objectives that challenge American interests, but doing so in a manner that does not require directly confronting China. This approach would make it easier for countries to partner in promoting a shared vision of the region without feeling as though their doing so would invite a bull's-eye on their back from Beijing. This approach places a higher priority on channeling Chinese ambitions into areas where the United States should welcome China's assuming greater responsibilities. It accepts that the United States has limited ability to decide events within China and focuses more on setting the regional environment within which China will rise. And it is grounded in greater confidence in America's enduring advantages in its competition with China.

America's toughest challenge is not China; it is finding a way to regain confidence that if the United States is open, prosperous, and true to its values, it has little to fear from Chinese competition, and indeed much to gain by serving as an inspiration for the world. As the China expert Evan Osnos has written, "The ascendant view in Washington holds that the competition is us-or-them; in fact, the reality of this century will be us-*and*-them. It is naïve to imagine wrestling China back to the past. The project, now, is to contest its moral vision of the future."[29]

George Kennan closed his two most seminal writings, the X article in *Foreign Affairs* and the Long Telegram from Embassy Moscow, with a call for the United States to live up to its own traditions and values. In the X article, Kennan wrote, "Thus the decision will really fall in large measure on this country itself. The issue of Soviet-American relations is in essence a test of the overall worth of the United States as a nation among nations. To avoid destruction the United States need only measure up to its own best traditions and prove itself worthy of preservation as a great nation."[30] And in the Long Telegram, he wrote, "Finally, we must have courage and self-confidence to cling to our own methods and conceptions of human society. After all, the greatest danger that can befall us in coping with this problem of Soviet communism is that we shall allow ourselves to become like those with whom we are coping."[31]

Although the circumstances of America's competition with China differ markedly from competition with the Soviet Union during the Cold War, the clarion call for the United States to outcompete China by improving itself remains as true today as it did then.

FOUR

Technology Competition

The United States is following a recognizable rhythm as it grows anxious about China's rapid economic rise, much as it has done throughout its history when it has encountered direct challenges to its economic standing. The sooner the United States accurately diagnoses the nature of the economic challenge China poses to American competitiveness, the better it will be able to mitigate risks of overreaction and instead concentrate on shoring up its own strengths. Arguably more so than military or geostrategic challenges, economic competition will form the core of rivalry between the United States and China well into the future. America's ability to outpace China in innovation is fundamental for sustaining its power and prestige in the international system. To do so, the United States' national-level government will need to restore its capacity for solving problems that are impeding America's economic dynamism.

Context

When the history of U.S.-China relations is written, the date September 27, 2019, may command a special significance. That is when

Huawei chief executive officer Ren Zhengfei announced that his company had begun producing 5G mobile base stations without any U.S. components. The announcement served as a symbolic middle finger to the United States, coming in the wake of an aggressive American campaign to undermine Huawei's competitive position. In the year before the announcement, the United States had launched a global effort to push other countries to sever business ties with Huawei, restricted sales of key U.S.-manufactured components to Huawei, barred Huawei from further penetration into the U.S. market, and, perhaps most personally troubling for Ren, compelled Canada to arrest his daughter for extradition to the United States to face criminal charges relating to Huawei's commercial activities with Iran. The U.S. strategy was supposed to cripple the company. Instead it caused the company to build new partnerships around the world, rely less on American components, and strive for self-sufficiency in advanced technologies. At a broader level, America's campaign against Huawei also demonstrated that instead of pushing China to become more liberal and market oriented, the United States was becoming more like China (that is, state led and security focused) in its pursuit of greater control over developments in the technology sector.

To be clear, I do not have sympathy for Huawei. While in government, I contributed to strategies to limit the reach of Huawei, particularly along America's periphery. Over the years, the company has abetted some of the most brutal regimes in the world by providing technologies to them that undermine American interests and values. The company maintains close connections with the top leadership in China. I fully expect that if compelled, the company would be responsive to Chinese requests for information on its users abroad.

Huawei's breakthrough on September 27, 2019, bears special significance not because of its success in bucking American pressure but because it may come to symbolize the date when the global technology industry split. It was not always this way. For many of the preceding decades, a largely symbiotic relationship prevailed between technology actors on the U.S. West Coast and China's eastern coast. U.S. tech companies would design and develop new products. Then they would outsource manufacturing and final assembly to China. The products would be marketed and sold around the world, generating revenue for the U.S. company that it would reinvest into research and development to spur the next generation of technology products and services that would get assembled in China. This virtuous cycle helped American information and communications technology companies spread their research and development costs over the largest possible number of global users, driving down costs and strengthening their competitive positions.[1]

The global technology industry now appears to be at risk of fracturing along the fault lines of intensifying competition between the United States and China. Now, each global power is seeking to reduce its dependence on the other, even as researchers and developers in the United States and China continue to collaborate in defiance of the darkening geostrategic clouds overhead.

Each country is pursuing selective decoupling from the other. This is manifesting in American directives to develop supply chains that do not include China for procuring items that are related to U.S. national security, broadly defined. Washington is also tightening export control restrictions, enhancing screening of inbound investment from China, scrutinizing Chinese students seeking to do research in the United States in science and technology fields, and throwing more resources at ferreting out Chinese attempts to acquire trade secrets and industrial designs through espionage.

Beijing is reciprocating in its efforts to limit vulnerabilities. Chinese authorities have announced plans to establish a "controlled entity list" for sensitive technologies. They have expanded industrial policies to accelerate their drive toward self-sufficiency in key sectors, tightened market access requirements in information technologies, strengthened censorship of content of American origin entering China, and increased scrutiny of American companies, individuals, and organizations operating in China. Beijing has also released a directive to remove American computers and software from government offices across the country.

The costs and consequences of these efforts by both sides to sever supply chains and reduce dependencies on each other, particularly in the technology sphere, could be significant. First, the more China progresses down the path of indigenous innovation and reduces its dependence on American imports of semiconductors and other components, the more impervious to American pressure Beijing will become. Second, government intervention in the flows of trade, technology, capital, and people will generate unintended second- and third-order effects that will harm American competitiveness. If Chinese students vote with their feet and choose to enroll in Australian and Canadian universities instead of American ones, for example, their choices will lead to lost revenues and budgetary pressures on American universities, to say nothing of lost innovation and missed opportunities for individual relationships to form across the Pacific. Already the percentage of Chinese overseas students choosing to study in the United States has begun declining as more Chinese students opt to go to Canada, Australia, and the United Kingdom instead. Third, nearly all economists agree that large-scale disruptions create inefficiencies, thereby increasing costs to consumers and lowering profits for companies.

The severing of trade and technology ties is not occurring in a vacuum. It is a symptom of a broader dynamic whereby each country is feeling increasingly vulnerable to the other. In the United States, one sees widely held concerns that China is rising at America's expense and is a cause of the economic malaise that many people are feeling.[2] This focus on China as the source of societal challenges in the United States is obscuring America's need to address its own domestic shortcomings.

Under President Trump, America's response to China's rise has been direct and unambiguous. The Trump administration has vowed to maintain America's economic primacy, and to use all available means to do so, including a wave of unilateralist protectionism against China unseen since the 1930s. Trump's strategy has been built on four interlocking assumptions: (1) the United States could impose sharp and targeted pain on China through unilateral tariffs; (2) China would bow to American demands for economic reform if faced with sufficient economic pressure; (3) a trade war with China is winnable at acceptable cost; and (4) American allies would support—and not seek to profit from—American pressure on China.

This campaign's ostensible goals were to compel China to amend its unfair trade practices, as outlined in the U.S. Trade Representative's Report to Congress under section 301 of the Trade Policy Act of 1974.[3] In practice, though, and in the comfort of quiet conversations, U.S. policy makers have readily acknowledged to me their underlying motivations: to slow down China's rise and reinvigorate the U.S. manufacturing sector. They saw trade activism against China as a means of pressuring companies to shift supply chains out of China, divest from China, and reinvest in the United States. President Trump often also fixated on the U.S. bilateral trade deficit with China.

Trump's narrow focus on the bilateral trade deficit made sense politically as a symbol of unfairness, but not strategically or economically. The deficit is a symptom of America's low savings rate, China's high savings rate, and U.S. competitive weakness in manufacturing and other tradable sectors.[4] Concentrating on the deficit number gave China leverage in negotiations to demand concessions from the United States in return for Chinese pledges to make big-ticket purchases of items China would have bought regardless.

At a broader level, the Trump administration's introduction of

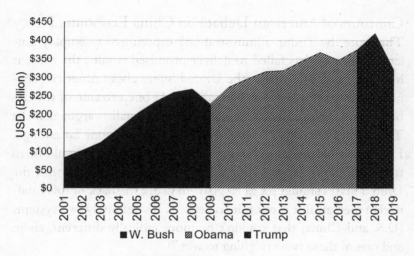

U.S. trade deficit with China, 2001–2019
Data from U.S. Census Bureau

unilateral tariffs triggered predictable Chinese retaliatory tariffs. The tit-for-tat tariffs have contributed to a spike in family farm foreclosures across the Midwest, along with the twin blow of a rise in suicides in those same communities.[5] The tariffs have caused many American companies that rely on imports of Chinese parts and components to see production costs rise and profits fall.

Simply put, America's reactively anxious response to China's rise is not delivering results that benefit hardworking Americans, solve global challenges, or strengthen American standing in the world. Instead, by unilaterally confronting China in hopes of slowing China's rise, the United States has validated a narrative inside China that America's actions are animated by insecurity about its relative decline. Such an approach has also triggered concern among America's allies and partners that the United States is lacking in leadership and losing its way—fearful of China's strength and forgetful of its own.

Contours of American Debate on China Economic Policy

The more the Trump administration's experiment to employ unilateral pressure has failed to deliver promised results, the more it has spurred debate within the United States about American economic policy responses to China's rise. At one extreme of the debate, Steve Bannon and other hard-right nationalists argue that the Trump administration's mistake is that it has not gone far enough. From their perspective, the objective of U.S. strategy should be to trigger regime change within China. In Bannon's own words, the United States should set as its goal "to break the back of this totalitarian mercantilist economic society. . . . It's definitely two systems [U.S. and China] that couldn't be more radically different, right, and one of these two are going to win."[6]

Another group of conservative voices has coalesced around the idea of "decoupling" the United States from China's economy. Proponents of this approach, such as former Trump White House senior director for strategic planning Robert Spaulding, argue that the United States needs to become more aggressive about starving China of the resources and know-how it needs to push toward the pinnacle of the global economy, while at the same time securing American supply chains by removing Chinese inputs from them.[7] Other conservatives, such as former politician Charles Boustany and Aaron Friedberg, a previous advisor to Vice President Cheney, believe that American interests can be protected through "partial disengagement" from China.[8] They assert that the United States should tighten screening of the outflow of technology to China, strengthen scrutiny of inbound Chinese investment and visitors, increase domestic investment in American innovation, and prioritize trade relationships with close allies.

Some members of the progressive Left and the nationalist Right argue that America's shortcoming is its inability to compete on a level playing field with China. Since China will not abandon its use of industrial policies to spur progress in key sectors, the United

States should adopt industrial policies of its own to negate China's advantages. Senators Marco Rubio and Elizabeth Warren disagree on most issues, but when it comes to promoting industrial policies to compete against China, they agree broadly.[9]

On the other end of the spectrum remains a group that believes the proper response to China's economic ascent is persistent engagement with China. Microsoft founder Bill Gates's views are representative of this group. Gates has decried the "paranoid" view fueling current policy efforts to decouple technology supply chains. He has warned that trying to stop Beijing from developing innovative technologies is "beyond realistic," and he has suggested that anyone who has any understanding of today's global innovation ecosystem would agree.[10]

And somewhere in the middle, a group of centrist voices acknowledge the intensifying competition with China and argue that the best American response would be to work with friends and allies around the world to set new rules and to outcompete China. Prominent voices such as Fareed Zakaria and Robert Zoellick argue in favor of a competitive coexistence with China.

America Has Been Here Before

While this mix of views on the most effective American response to China's technological and economic ascent may seem messy in the moment, it is worth recalling that in many ways it is in keeping with America's political tradition. Since the founding of the republic, the United States has developed a pattern of heightened sensitivity to foreign economic challengers. America has often responded initially to foreign economic challengers with clouded policy judgments and disruptive behaviors before eventually settling into efforts to outpace competitors.

As the trade expert Jonathan Hillman has recounted, at the dawn of the nineteenth century, Americans were worried that the British had a vast plot to destroy U.S. industry, weaken the new country, and reassert control over the former colonies. Widespread rumors circulated of British agents sabotaging American industry across the newfound states, from farms in Connecticut to factories in Philadelphia. In response, the United States launched an array of efforts to safeguard its economic security from foreign meddling.[11]

Similar fears warped U.S. policy debates between the Civil War and World War I, and then again in the 1930s, when the media magnate William Randolph Hearst used his megaphone to rally for a ban on Asian products entering the American market. Shortly thereafter, the Smoot-Hawley Tariff Act was enacted. The law raised import duties to protect American business and farmers from "unfair" international competition and, in the process, significantly exacerbated the effects of the Great Depression.

A similar reflex reappeared in the 1980s, spurred by Japan's seemingly unrelenting economic rise. Both then and after the Soviet Union's launch of *Sputnik* three decades earlier, the United States exhibited a profound anxiety about whether it could compete against a state-guided model for scientific innovation.

America's charges against Japan for economic unfairness in the 1980s are strikingly similar to criticisms of Chinese misdeeds today. As the foreign policy expert Fareed Zakaria has recounted, "At the time, Clyde Prestowitz's influential book *Trading Places: How America Is Surrendering Its Future to Japan and How to Win It Back* explained that the United States had never imagined dealing with a country in which 'industry and trade [would be] organized as part of an effort to achieve specific national goals.' Another widely read book of the era was titled *The Coming War with Japan*. As Japanese growth tapered off, so did these exaggerated fears."[12]

In all these instances, the initial American response was to pin blame on the cunning and corner-cutting ways of foreigners who were building advantage over honest and hardworking Americans. The United States has also often shown a bias toward assuming that foreign competitors were marching in lockstep in furtherance of a cohesive national strategy to dominate global markets at America's expense. During certain periods, such as the anti-Japan backlash of the 1980s, the reaction of the American public was to smash Japanese cars, televisions, and video recorders in public protests. Racism, nationalism, and xenophobia have often accompanied these bouts of anxiety about America's economic competitiveness.

Tariffs have frequently been the tool of first choice for responding to external economic competition. Think of the Smoot-Hawley tariffs, the Buy American Act of 1933, and trade restrictions on Japanese imports in the 1980s. In the last case, deputy U.S. trade representative Robert Lighthizer negotiated a set of voluntary restraint agreements with Japan that limited the number of vehicles Japan would import to the United States. This incentivized Japan to maximize profits on the limited numbers of cars it could sell in the U.S. market, compelling Japanese companies to move into the luxury market that had previously been dominated by American car companies like Cadillac and Oldsmobile. Japanese luxury brands such as Lexus, Infiniti, and Acura owe part of their success to policy manifestations of American anxiety during that period.

I make these points not to draw easily disputable parallels between the China of today and previous economic competitors. One can draw many fundamental distinctions between China's actions and ambitions, its governmental character, and its relationship with the United States relative to those earlier periods. My main point is to highlight the consistency of the United States' reflexive pattern of reactions to external economic challengers.

The typical rhythm of American behavior involves a sharp initial reaction, tempered later by a more focused identification of challenges and a more balanced approach to addressing them. I expect this latest bout with China to follow a similar pattern. But how fast the United States cycles through its pattern of behavior will depend on two factors: (1) how quickly the United States develops a serious diagnosis of the nature of current economic competition with China;

and (2) how quickly it coalesces political and public support behind a strategy for strengthening its own competitiveness to meet the challenges presented by China.

Diagnosing U.S.-China Economic Relations

A popular American narrative is that China's unfair activities are destroying America's economy and potentially imperiling its national security. America's concerns about Chinese behavior have been amplified by China's declared ambitions to become the world leader in a whole range of areas, from electric vehicles to artificial intelligence, semiconductors, and robotics.[13] And China's efforts to bolster the development of dual-use technologies through "integrated development" between the civilian and security sectors have led many American defense planners to worry that China's economic advances are intensifying the military threat.[14]

This popular diagnosis of the U.S.-China economic relationship offers little, however, in explaining how the United States and China are relating to each other in the global economy, or how the two economies might develop alongside each other going forward. Understanding U.S.-China economic relations today requires holding two seemingly contradictory thoughts simultaneously. First, the United States and China are the two behemoths of the international system. Both are widening the distance between themselves and every other country in the world in terms of economic size, pace of innovation, and overall national power. Second, China's future economic outlook has many uncertainties. The one near-certainty is that China's economy will not continue growing at the same breakneck speed that it has enjoyed in recent decades.

Even as the rate of China's economic growth decelerates, the size of China's contribution to global economic growth will remain extremely large, because China is growing from a larger base (and percentage of global GDP) than in the past. With a high savings rate, potential to produce more value-added content in global supply chains, and a still relatively low per capita income (approximately $10,000), China has room to grow. China certainly faces strong economic headwinds that will cause its rate of growth to cool relative to its own past performance, but even as it does so, it will likely remain the fastest-growing part of the world economy. In other words, a cooling economy does not equate to a collapsing one.

The United States and China: Separating from the Pack

The United States and China are the only two countries in human history with economies that have surpassed $10 trillion in nominal gross domestic product. Put together, the two economies now account for nearly 40 percent of global GDP. While the world is becoming more multipolar on security issues, it is increasingly bipolar in the technology world.

The United States and China are navigating the frontier of innovation simultaneously. As the Microsoft executives Brad Smith and Carol Ann Browne have observed, "China and the United States are the world's two largest consumers of information technology. They have also become the two largest suppliers of this technology to the rest of the world. On many days, a scan of the stock market listings will show that seven of the world's ten most valuable companies are technology enterprises. Five of these seven are American, while the other two are Chinese."[15] Further illustrating the point, the Atlantic Council predicts that by 2030 a hierarchical order of technology innovation will have emerged, with only the United States and China at the pinnacle, other advanced economies lagging behind, and everyone else lost in the background.[16]

China Is Facing Economic Headwinds

As briefly discussed in chapter 1, although China's four-decade run of rapid economic growth has been historic, its future economic outlook is far from certain. For starters, China has already squeezed out most of the benefits of its transition from a state-directed economy toward a market-based economy. China's traditional drivers of growth are running out of steam. As a group of leading American and Chinese economists have concluded, "China's years of continuous 10 percent or even 8 percent economic growth are over permanently. Government officials and private entrepreneurs should be prepared, both psychologically and economically, for this long-term decline of growth rates."[17]

China's economy faces important discontinuities from its recent past. First, China no longer enjoys low-cost production advantages over competitors. Second, China can no longer afford to treat its air and water as expendable resources. China has accrued significant welfare losses as a result of environmental degradation during its rapid economic expansion. Higher environmental standards will likely place a drag on GDP growth. Third, China faces a more uncertain external economic environment. Over recent decades, China's rise has coincided with a period of global economic liberalization. Now those trends show signs of reversing as the United States and others put up higher protectionist walls. And fourth, demographics are moving from a net benefit to a net drag on China's economy. The dependency ratio, which measures the proportion of non-working-age population to total population, could rise to 66 percent in 2049, while the working-age population could shrink by up to 170 million people between 2019 and 2049. This growing bulge of the population entering retirement will weaken consumption demand and squeeze government resources as more people demand better social safety net benefits.[18]

These challenges are unlikely to be offset by productivity gains. Over the past decade, total factor productivity has become relatively flat. To spur greater productivity, Chinese authorities could improve the efficiency in allocation of resources, further open the economy to foreign competition, and strengthen intellectual property protections to better incentivize innovation.[19] To date, progress on these fronts has been uneven.

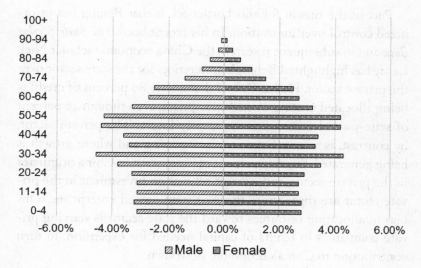

China population pyramid, 2019
Data from United Nations, Department of Economic and Social Affairs,
Population Division

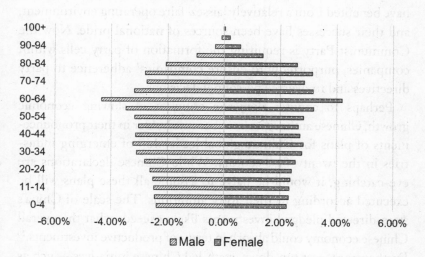

China population pyramid, 2050
Data from United Nations, Department of Economic and Social Affairs,
Population Division

Part of the reason for this bottleneck is that Beijing has prioritized control over innovation. In his recent book *The State Strikes Back* and in subsequent research, the China economic scholar Nick Lardy has highlighted Beijing's preferences for the state sector over the private sector. He has shown that nearly 80 percent of credit is being allocated to state-owned enterprises, even though 40 percent of state-owned enterprises are money losers. The private sector, by contrast, is where dynamism is occurring and where growth is being generated. Seventy percent of innovation in China originates in the private sector, and average returns on investment in the private sector are three times those of state-owned enterprises. This bias in allocating resources toward the state sector is starving private companies in China of capital needed for expansion, in turn contributing to China's economic slowdown.

Moreover, the Chinese Communist Party is reasserting political control over companies in China, including private technology companies. For the past decade, Chinese technology companies have benefited from a relatively laissez-faire operating environment, and their successes have been sources of national pride. Now the Communist Party is requiring the formation of party cells within companies, purportedly to ensure companies' adherence to party directives and to oversee personnel decisions.

Perhaps to counter domestic criticism of slowing economic growth, Chinese authorities have become bolder in their pronouncements of plans for Chinese global leadership of emerging industries in the twenty-first century. While Chinese declarations are eye-catching, it would be naive to assume all these plans will be executed according to their lofty ambitions. The scale of China's state-directed pledged investments likely exceeds what the overall Chinese economy could absorb in terms of productive investments.[20] Furthermore, past top-down, state-led Chinese initiatives—such as for new-energy vehicles, semiconductors, and commercial aircraft—

have had uneven records of success.[21] They have often led to waste, fraud, duplication, and overcapacity.

The more China advances state-directed efforts to spur innovation, the more it will be placing its bureaucrats in competition with American venture capitalists. When bureaucrats are responsible for allocating funds, they must weigh the risk of having their careers derailed by failed investments. This skews allocation of capital toward safe bets, for example national champions and state-owned enterprises. And the more Chinese firms are incentivized to focus on indigenous innovation and top-down directives, the less reliant they will be on the open, transnational innovation models that have sparked breakthroughs and new technologies. Whereas much of the rest of the global economy is moving toward internationally integrated supply chains that exploit comparative advantages in different corners of the world, China is moving in the opposite direction as it seeks to indigenize a greater share of its production, ostensibly to secure its sources of inputs and minimize supply disruptions. China cannot draw on historical precedents for gaining comparative advantage by increasing autarky.

The upshot of these twin developments—the United States and China racing ahead of the pack even as China encounters economic headwinds—is that both countries will remain central actors in the international system for the foreseeable future. Both the OECD and PricewaterhouseCoopers (PwC) forecast that U.S. and Chinese GDP growth rates will increasingly converge over time as China loses its low-cost advantages and transitions from input-driven to innovation-driven growth.[22] In present circumstances, with both countries acting as the twin engines of the global economy and simultaneously trading over $700 billion in goods and services between them, it defies the imagination to conceive of a scenario whereby one country rises while the other one falls, even as both countries presently strive to selectively decouple in national security-sensitive sectors.

Contra the popular narrative in the United States, China's recent economic growth has not come at America's expense. In fact, America's share of global GDP has remained relatively steady over the past two decades, even as China's has risen rapidly. The key shifts have occurred in Europe and Japan, both of whose shares of global output have dropped while China's has risen.

Furthermore, the difference between U.S. and Chinese nominal GDP has remained relatively flat since 2013, at around $7 trillion. Even if China closes this gap in the coming years and reaches parity with or exceeds America in terms of economic output, the spoils of this success will need to be spread across a population four times that of the United States. These facts are important not because they provide grounds for complacency but because they offer a corrective to occasional waves of defeatism in the United States that "China is eating our lunch." The Chinese are making giant strides, but their progress has not necessarily come at America's expense.

Why Outpacing China in Technology Innovation Matters

The next wave of technology breakthroughs will generate economic and military advantages for the country that develops and deploys them first. That is why technology competition—more so than military arms racing or ideological expansionism—will form the core of U.S.-China competition in the twenty-first century. To go a step further, America's ability to outpace the competition and preserve its innovation edge matters for four primary reasons.

The first is the pull of power that comes from being an exemplar of sustained success. For more than seventy years, the United States has maintained its position as the leading technologically innovative power. This has contributed to one of America's most important and least quantifiable strengths: the power of global attraction for its economic and political system. It is hardly coincidental that the current global democratic recession is occurring at a time when

America's model is showing signs of fatigue while China's statist system appears to be delivering social stability and economic growth. Absent a course correction, this trend could usher in an era where countries increasingly turn to China's governance experience for ideas on how to address their own domestic challenges.

Second, maintaining an edge matters for purposes of rule setting. China's efforts to amend the international system are playing out in ways both large and small, ranging from setting technical standards for 5G technologies to questions about internet governance and rules on cross-border data flows. The country that sets the pace in innovation will also be the country that has the inside track in setting rules and standards that favor its technologies in the global marketplace.

The third reason is national security. Increasingly, foundational technologies have dual-use civilian and military applications. Autonomous systems, machine learning, quantum computing, and biotechnology, for example, all have clear military applications. The more the United States builds an edge in these emerging technologies, the more it will be able to engage China and other rivals from a position of strength and confidence. Greater self-confidence could help dampen American impulses toward seeking to subvert China's advances, thereby reducing risk of direct confrontation.

The fourth reason is America's standing in Asia and globally. Increasingly, economic—not security—issues are the coin of the realm. The stronger America's innovation output, the greater America's appeal. And this matters greatly. As the development expert Homi Kharas has shown, Asia is now home to half of the twenty fast-growing economies, generates two-thirds of global growth, and accounts for 40 percent of global GDP. Sixty percent of the world's population lives in the continent, and the size of Asia's middle class (notably including China and India) is expected to reach 2.3 billion people, or 65 percent of the world's total, by 2030.[23] While people around the world and across Asia respect America's military strength, they are often more inspired by America's capacity for creation.

How to Maintain the Edge: Concentrate at Home, Strengthen Rules Abroad

During the Trump administration, significant national focus and government resources have been devoted to slowing China down. President Trump has touted progress along these lines by claiming credit for having caused China's economy to experience its "worst year" in fifty-seven years (a claim that has not held up under fact-checking scrutiny).[24]

Rather than fixating on slowing down China, future American leaders will also need to focus on speeding up American advances. The hard reality is that only China will be able to slow down China's rise, just as only America will determine America's future course. Former World Bank president Robert Zoellick summed up the sentiment well: "The best U.S. response to China's innovation agenda is to strengthen our own capabilities and to draw the world's talent, ideas, entrepreneurs, and venture capital to its [U.S.] shores. We will succeed by facing up to our own flaws."[25]

Since my focus is on effectively managing U.S.-China relations, and not on renewing America's economic strength, I will not detour too far into discussing what America needs to do to improve its own economic condition. But I will make a few observations that support my broader argument that America should have confidence in its ability to compete with China.

Six Steps to Strengthen American Competitiveness

The steps America needs to take to enhance its economic competitiveness are not much of a mystery or source of debate. Many of the challenges the U.S. economy confronts today are not new and are not being imposed on the United States from abroad. In fact, many of them were presciently forecast by a young advisor to Richard Nixon in 1971. At that time, Pete Peterson wrote a 133-page memo titled "The United States in a Changing World Economy." The memo warned of major discontinuities resulting from globalization but argued that the major sources of American economic challenges were homegrown. Peterson argued that prosperity in the new era of global competition "depends mainly *on our own efforts* rather than on the actions of other countries." He called on the United States to undertake a comprehensive effort to "increase our competitiveness, our productivity and, in general, enlarge the areas of comparative advantage vis-à-vis the rest of the world. The way to do this is to concentrate on the things we do best. This in turn will increase our international competitiveness."

To do so, leaders in government, business, and academia will need to rebuild bipartisan consensus around the principle that the United States will be stronger by preserving openness than by becoming closed in vain pursuit of absolute security against all external threats.

Openness is one of America's core advantages in competition with China. In recent years, Beijing has intensified efforts to tighten its oversight of the flow of ideas and information inside China, ostensibly for purposes of strengthening social control. It remains to be seen whether China can become a truly innovative society at the same time as it asserts ever-tighter political control.

On the flip side, leading American innovators such as Harry Shum, former Microsoft executive vice president of artificial intelligence and research, have shared with me the benefits that companies like Microsoft derive from connection to global teams of innovators contributing to a shared creation process. It is precisely the open flow of ideas, information, and individuals that has spurred so many technological breakthroughs at leading American firms like Microsoft, Google, and Facebook.

America's open, democratic system has also been a beacon for many of the best minds around the world. Just look at the large share of Nobel Prizes that American immigrants have been awarded, or the fact that half of the nation's Fields Medals for outstanding achievement in mathematics have been won by immigrants. Sixty percent of the most highly valued technology companies today were founded by immigrants or children of immigrants, including eBay, Intel, and Google.[26] Understanding these realities and concerned that the United States could turn its back on one of its strongest advantages, MIT president L. Rafael Reif wrote, "If all we do in response to China's ambition is try to double-lock all our doors, I believe we will lock ourselves into mediocrity."[27]

Second, and relatedly, broad support for continued openness will require increased investment in America's social safety net. Although free trade has been broadly positive for America's economy, the costs and benefits of increased globalization have not been distributed evenly. While the exact number of manufacturing job losses owing to trade with China is a subject of dispute, the broader point is not.[28] Many workers have been affected negatively by globalization and automation, and many of those workers associate their frustrations with China.

Fortunately, other nations have developed ways to address this problem. As the foreign policy commentator Kishore Mahbubani has argued, "Many societies, from Sweden to Singapore, have devised various social safety nets to help the working classes handle the disruptions of globalization."[29] They recognize that free trade is not free. Likewise, the United States will need to improve the quality of its investments in social welfare if it wants to fireproof itself against isolationist domestic political pressures to seek shelter from external challenges by turning away from the world.

Third, the U.S. government will need to restore funding for basic scientific research to its historical average. According to one estimate, "This would mean increasing funding from 0.7 to 1.1 percent of gross domestic product annually, or from $146 billion to about $230 billion (in 2018 dollars)."[30]

Some may argue that America does not need such investments, particularly in fiscally constrained times, because the bulk of R&D funding now comes from the American private sector. The problem with this logic is that U.S. companies over time are spending less on basic research and more on development of marketable products.[31] Corporate R&D funding typically focuses on later-stage research with clearer odds of delivering return on investment. Only the federal government can fill the growing gap in funding for basic research, and at this moment, it is failing to do so. As a result, innovations that were sparked by government-funded basic research in previous generations (for example, the microchip, the semiconductor laser, plasma displays, and the internet) are not coming online now. The longer this trend persists, the more the United States risks lagging in its capacity to pioneer groundbreaking technology.

Additionally, the United States should expand basic research partnership arrangements with its closest international partners, including its Five Eyes intelligence-sharing partners (the United

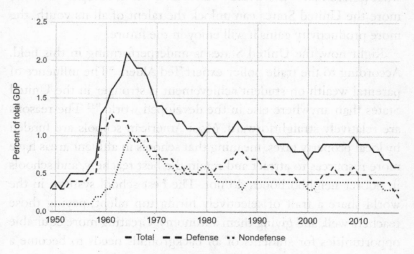

U.S. government historical R&D spending, 1949–2018
Data from U.S. Office of Management and Budget

Kingdom, Canada, Australia, and New Zealand), as well as Japan, on basic and applied research. This approach would help spread the costs over a wider base, relieving the budgetary burden on the U.S. government during a period of intensifying competition for discretionary resources.

Fourth, the U.S. government needs to develop incentives that will help to restore the so-called iron triangle of innovation between government, academia, and the private sector. Vannevar Bush helped build this research triangle in the 1940s. In the ensuing decades, it paid dividends, helping to realize Bush's vision of "pushing frontiers of mind." Bush forecast that the innovation triangle would generate jobs, improve standards of living, and strengthen national security. He was right. U.S. society must relearn how to fire on all cylinders again, as opposed to keeping new ideas cordoned off in private labs for the sole purpose of maximizing profit.

Fifth, the United States needs to prioritize efforts to create more equal opportunities for academic advancement. Human capital is what differentiates the United States from all its competitors. The more the United States can unlock the talent of all its youth, the more productivity gains it will enjoy in the future.

Right now, the United States is underperforming in this field. According to the trade policy expert Ted Alden, "The influence of parental wealth on student achievement is stronger in the United States than anywhere else in the developed world."[32] The reasons are relatively straightforward. Most American schools are funded by local property taxes, meaning that schools in affluent areas have more resources to attract and retain the best teachers, and schools in poorer neighborhoods do not. The best school systems in the world share a trait of selectively hiring top talent, paying those teachers well, and giving them autonomy. Creating more equitable opportunities for students of all backgrounds needs to become a priority in the United States.

Last, the United States needs to strengthen its defenses against leakage or theft of cutting-edge and dual-use technology to China and other competitors. It can do so through enhanced foreign investment screening, updated export controls that are synchronized with other advanced economies, and improved counterespionage efforts. In all these areas, the key priority is to preserve America's openness to the maximum extent possible.

An absolute effort to restrict the export of all sensitive technology to China would cede the Chinese market to other countries that might have fewer compunctions about trade relations with China, as occurred when the United States previously sought to restrict sales of machine tools and satellites. A more successful approach would be to coordinate with other like-minded countries to control the export of emerging and foundational technologies to Chinese end users of concern. By restricting transfers only to Chinese end users that pose a security risk or have a proven track record of complicity in human rights violations, this approach would strike a balance that serves U.S. innovation. It would not eliminate the risk of U.S. technology falling into the wrong hands in China, but practically speaking, neither would any other approach short of a full embargo of American-origin products to China. Even in that extreme circumstance, there would almost certainly still be carve-outs and illicit third-country transfers of American technology to China.[33]

While I could cite bookshelves filled with additional ideas for strengthening America's innovation edge—for example, upgrading infrastructure, strengthening antimonopoly enforcement, and so on—my illustrative examples here are intended to show that much of what needs to be done is well within reach and at manageable costs to American taxpayers. Even without additional suggestions, I am confident these steps on their own would be enough to outpace China in the ongoing technology innovation race.

Writing the Rules of the Road

While the bulk of effort in outcompeting China will necessarily need to focus on domestic renewal, there is also an international component. Since the end of World War II, the United States has traditionally been a leading player—arguably *the* leading player—in developing rules, norms, and institutions. From the United Nations to the Bretton Woods system, the World Trade Organization, and the Paris Agreement, the United States has exercised outsize influence over the international system relative to all other nations. In recent years, that pattern has begun to shift as China has increasingly shown interest in convening countries, advancing its own initiatives, and placing its citizens in leadership positions of international bodies.

The United States needs to revive its rules-making muscles lest it become disadvantaged by regulations drafted in Beijing that give Chinese firms advantages over their American competitors. Ideally, the United States would rejoin the Comprehensive and Progressive Agreement for Trans-Pacific Partnership and join an updated version of the European Union–Japan free economic partnership agreement, agreements that would anchor two-thirds of the global economy to the same high standards and rules as America's own system. If such a step proves politically untenable, as it appears at this moment, the United States could also take interim steps with its partners to shape China's incentives for reform. These steps could include cooperating with like-minded countries to develop common standards and policies for the use and control of emerging technologies. They could involve a concerted effort at the World Trade Organization to tighten subsidy rules and link them to trade penalties. They could also involve more ambitious efforts to build rules around data flows. For example, Ian Bremmer, founder of the Eurasia Group, has proposed that the United States lead efforts to launch a World Data Organization that helps set and enforce international standards for data, privacy, and intellectual property.[34]

These examples illustrate a broader point: being a rule setter has inherent advantages, international rules are lacking in many areas, and if the United States does not exercise leadership along with its partners to address these shortcomings, then China will.

America's Biggest Challenge Is Itself

The most significant challenge confronting the United States is not what China is doing or the absence of a strategy for dealing with China. It is America's national-level political system. The national political system currently is not solving problems, even when the problems are fixable and the solutions are known. As the commentator Peter Beinart has observed, "Over the past two decades, American politicians have not proved weak and inert in responding to China's real and imagined misdeeds. They have proved weak and inert in responding to their own citizens' needs. The reckoning Washington requires is not with China. It's with itself."[35]

Modern history offers virtually no examples of a country sustaining a thriving economy with a dysfunctional political system.[36] Ultimately what separates thriving societies from failing ones is the quality of the institutions and their capacity to solve problems. The contrasts between South Korea and North Korea today, or between West Germany and East Germany in past decades, provide living proof of this point.

When national-level leaders with a commitment to practical problem-solving reemerge, they will encounter many areas of low-hanging fruit. For example, the U.S. government could achieve high-impact, high-payoff investments by rebuilding its crumbling infrastructure and making it more resilient to weather-driven events, building out national digital infrastructure, providing effective job training to displaced workers, investing in prekindergarten education, expanding coverage for preventive health care, and implementing existing antitrust laws to stimulate innovation. Any of these steps would not only improve America's economic competitiveness but also support America's psychological strengthening. It would provide fresh optimism to American citizens that the United States remains capable of moving forward, rather than simply remaining stuck in place while elected leaders take partisan shots at one another.

Even as the national-level political system has degenerated, though, it is worth recalling that a lot of energy and activism remains at the subnational level. Local-level governments have been taking the lead in responding to COVID-19 when the national government has fallen short. They have also been launching training programs, incubating local venture capital funds to encourage start-ups, and traveling the world to attract foreign investment and promote exports. These efforts have crossed party lines, with Democratic and Republican governors and mayors taking on activist roles. And they have proved that creativity and initiative remain abundant across the United States, if not necessarily in Washington, D.C.

These examples give us grounds for optimism that the United States remains capable of addressing its deficiencies going forward. The best reason for optimism is that it is possible to identify policies to restore America's strength, revive the power of its example to the world, and protect America's innovation edge.

The United States today is the same country that delivered world-changing innovations from garages in Seattle and Palo Alto in previous decades that led to the creation of global brands like Microsoft, Google, and Amazon. These innovations were not fueled by government direction or top-down mandate. They were enabled by a creative and ambitious group of individuals who had access to capital, an ability to attract global talent, and space to grow their companies in an environment that had reasonable competition policy.

The United States does not need to bifurcate the global technology sector and squeeze Chinese competitors to protect its edge. It does not need to compete by becoming more like China. America can answer challenges from China by improving its own condition. On this score, the United States still has plenty of room to realize progress and reach its national potential.

FIVE

Mitigating Risks of Conflict

It is possible to be clear-eyed about the profound risks to peace in East Asia without falling into lazy assumptions about the inevitability of conflict between the United States and China in the process. Just as there are acute risks, so there are also ample areas where the United States could improve its ability to deter Chinese threats. Most important, both countries have strong incentives to avoid conflict. Prioritizing *risk reduction* in areas of ongoing contestation and *norm building* in areas of emerging technology competition holds the greatest promise for the world's two leading powers to chart a path forward that allows for competition and limits risk of conflict.

Context

A little over a century ago, a senior official in the British Foreign Office wrote a piercing analysis of the implications of Germany's rise for the United Kingdom's security and prosperity. The official, Sir Eyre Crowe, sought to sound the alarm against British complacency toward Germany's military buildup, particularly its rapid expansion in naval capabilities, which were developing along a trajectory that would soon challenge Britain's dominance of the high seas. Crowe's memorandum, delivered on New Year's Day 1907, warned that conflict was inherent in the shifting balance of power between the United Kingdom and Germany. He concluded that once Germany achieved naval supremacy over the United Kingdom, regardless of its stated intentions, Germany would pose a dire threat and be "incompatible with the existence of the British Empire."[1]

Seven years before the outbreak of World War I, Crowe had determined that conflict would be the mechanical result of irreconcilable geostrategic stresses between two strong and ambitious powers. Sadly, his predictions were borne out in one of the most violent conflicts of modern history.

Fast-forward to the present day, and the parallels with the United States and China are uncomfortably close. Like the United Kingdom at the dawn of the twentieth century, the United States today sustains its geostrategic advantage in part through its global naval capacity, which enables the United States to project force and maintain presence in virtually every corner of the world. This capability sets America apart from every other country and contributes to its unmatched international influence.

And like Germany at the dawn of the twentieth century, China is translating its rapid economic gains into the creation of a formidable military force. In raw numerical terms, China's PLA Navy has already surpassed the U.S. Navy by a count of hulls. Even so, China's naval capabilities remain significantly behind those of the United States, not only in quality but also in combined fleet tonnage, given the large size of many American ships.[2]

Nevertheless, China's significant investments in instruments for projecting power beyond its shores have led to a growing chorus of American experts who treat as a foregone conclusion that China seeks to dominate Asia and displace the United States as the leading global superpower. This viewpoint has become embroidered into

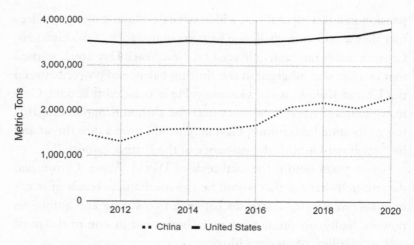

U.S.-China naval vessel tonnage comparisons, 2010–2020
Data from *Jane's Fighting Ships*, International Institute for Strategic Studies

the speech patterns of American politicians of both major political parties, including Democratic senator Mark Warner, Republican senator Marco Rubio, and Vice President Pence and Secretary of State Pompeo.

Many foreign policy realists such as John Mearsheimer have been predicting this moment for some time. They have argued that an ascendant China will try to use its growing influence to remake the international system to better serve China's own interests. In this view, the tectonic shifts set off by China's rise will lead to an epic battle over primacy in Asia and leadership of the international system. Harvard professor Graham Allison has similarly warned about risks of rising powers coming into conflict with established powers, a concept he has popularized as the "Thucydides trap."

At the moment, such viewpoints are influential within the American policy and analytic communities. And as the über-realist Henry Kissinger has warned, "Whatever China's intentions, the Crowe school of thought would treat a successful Chinese 'rise' as incompatible with America's position in the Pacific and by extension the world."[3]

While China's conduct has contributed significantly to the ascendance of the Crowe school of thought within America's expert and policy community, there also is an ideological element that has roots in America's analytic tradition. In recent decades, it has become an article of faith for many American policy makers and analysts, particularly among neoconservatives and grand strategists, to view a country's governance model as being highly relevant to the type of relationship it has with the United States. According to this argument, democratic institutions are more conducive to relationships of trust and confidence, and nondemocratic institutions are not. The latter are inherently brittle, precarious, and prone to the exercise of force, both to suppress their own citizens and to seize initiative against those that challenge their interests abroad. Therefore, as Kissinger distills the argument, "The United States is obliged to exercise its maximum influence (in its polite expression) or pressure to bring about more pluralistic institutions where they do not exist, and especially in countries capable of threatening American security. In these conceptions, regime change is the ultimate goal of American foreign policy in dealing with nondemocratic societies; peace with China is less a matter of strategy than of change in Chinese governance."[4]

These views are not mere abstractions. I have repeatedly encountered in consultations with policy makers and experts a belief that U.S. policy must be organized to compel the Chinese Communist Party to change in fundamental ways or cede its one-party rule of China—in effect, to change or die. Chinese officials are aware of these impulses in American foreign policy. Chinese officials fear that their American counterparts see an irreconcilability between the existence of the Chinese Communist Party and America's preferred conception of the world. Even when elected American leaders do not hold ideological hostility toward them, such views are always only one election away from resurfacing. Chinese leaders are not entirely wrong in this concern.

U.S. Capacity for Influencing Chinese Behavior

Many who have firsthand experience in managing the relationship over the past forty years, myself included, do not interpret China as being on an inexorable rise and do not subscribe to the ahistorical trope that China's external behavior is impervious to influence by incentives or threats from abroad. Previous policy practitioners ranging from Henry Kissinger to Susan Rice, Steve Hadley, Stapleton Roy, Jeff Bader, and Ken Lieberthal, among others, recognize the constant strategic interaction between the United States and China, wherein both sides make national policies and choices in an interactive manner, each responding to the thrusts and parries of the other while working to manage security dilemmas along the way. They do not share the view that China is single-mindedly united behind a coherent strategy for reaching a predetermined destination by persisting down a preset path. In other words, the type of mechanical thinking that defines the Crowe school of thought does not hold explanatory or predictive value for many previous policy makers who have held responsibility for actually conducting the relationship.

I have watched firsthand on many occasions how U.S. diplomacy has affected China's behavior. Credible threats of U.S. sanctions compelled China to alter its practices on government-sponsored cyber-enabled economic espionage from 2015 to 2016. An authoritative warning about possible military conflict caused China to pull back from conducting land reclamation at Scarborough Shoal in the South China Sea in 2016 and to dial back its naval blockade on Philippine-occupied Second Thomas Shoal one year earlier. Similarly, China shifted from opposing to supporting sanctions against North Korea in the United Nations Security Council in 2016 when the costs and risks of obstruction were put in stark relief for Chinese leaders. A similar process a decade earlier prompted China to convene the Six-Party Talks on North Korean denuclearization. Going back further, a combination of threats and inducements compelled China to move from being the world's leading proliferator to joining other global powers in working to uphold nonproliferation norms.

This is not to suggest that China acts like an ally in addressing American security concerns. It surely does not. Nor do I suggest that the United States has gotten its way with China every time it has put its mind to it. That has not been the case.

Rather, my point is to highlight that it remains possible to influence China's national choices. The Trump administration's paltry record in influencing China's policy decisions through unilateral threats paired with presidential obsequiousness is not evidence of America's inability to shape China's choices. The Trump administration was dealing with the same Chinese leadership team that just years earlier had altered its behavior on cyber-enabled economic espionage for commercial gain under heightened diplomatic pressure and credible threats of economic sanctions. It was working with the same Chinese leaders who had joined with the United States to seal the Paris Agreement and had partnered with the United States to stamp out Ebola in East Africa.

If skeptics of America's ability to shape China's decisions are unpersuaded by previous administrations' records with China, they can also look back at President Reagan's record with the Soviet Union. Despite deep divisions between Washington and Moscow over ideology and values and conflicting geostrategic ambitions, Reagan succeeded in eliciting meaningful cooperation with the Soviet Union on various American priorities, most notably arms control, while standing firmly for American values. Reagan understood the power of framing American values as an aspiration, rather than as a tool for attacking opponents.

All countries are guided by their identification of national interests. China is no different. China remains responsive to incentives and disincentives. Hard-nosed U.S. diplomacy backed by all other elements of American national power remains capable of influencing Beijing's external behavior.

The Most Likely Future Scenario: Heightened Competition, Not Conflict

My experiences lead me to the strong conviction that no mechanical formula is capable of determining that the U.S.-China relationship is fated to follow some predetermined path toward heightened confrontation and eventual conflict. To the contrary, I believe the United States and China are fated to coexist within a state of heightened rivalry and competition. Here is why.

First, neither the United States nor China will be capable of dominating Asia at the other's expense; both will have to live alongside each other. The regional security landscape in East Asia is not a two-player game between the United States and China. Rather, it encompasses arguably the most crowded strategic space in the world. China faces Russia in the north and Russia's traditional sphere of influence in the west. India sits to its south. Vietnam and its capable submarine fleet reside next door. Indonesia and Malaysia are not far away. North Korea, South Korea, and Japan watch every Chinese move warily from the east. Taiwan has ramped up its purchases of advanced weapons systems to complicate Chinese war planning for any cross-Strait contingency. And the U.S. armed forces maintain a constant presence off China's coastline 365 days per year. China has more nuclear-armed neighbors than any other country in the world. It faces what may be the most complex and challenging external environment of any major country.

Second, China will become increasingly occupied by domestic challenges in the years to come, which will limit its capacity to pursue a purely confrontational policy toward the United States. Beijing is attempting to achieve something no other country has before: to transform its economy with an aging society and a massive debt load. In the safety of closed-door conversations, Chinese leaders often acknowledge to American counterparts that they have their hands full with domestic challenges, and those challenges occupy the bulk of their mental bandwidth. Indeed, this was the running theme of unscripted discussions between Obama and Xi when they met for meals on the margins of summits. Further, China does not have a modern historical precedent of launching external aggression to distract from domestic challenges (the wag-the-dog scenario). The opposite has been the case.

Third, military conflict is not a viable option for either side to impose its will over the other. The United States and China each possess weapons of mass destruction, as well as modern military technologies of sweeping destructive capacity. Unlike leaders in London and Berlin before World War I, today we no longer have any uncertainty about the scale of destruction that would be unleashed in the event of conflict. Nobody now could credibly argue that conflict between the United States and China could be conducted on the cheap or that it would remain localized to East Asia. As a consequence, premeditated great power conflict has become a virtual impossibility. This has eliminated conflict as the tool that rising powers had previously relied on to wrest dominance away from declining hegemonic states.

Fourth, human agency is involved in decisions of war. Up to now, every American and Chinese leader has viewed avoiding military conflict as being in his country's interests. No public enthusiasm exists in either country for conflict. To the contrary, broad constituencies in both countries would dramatically be negatively affected by conflict.

Fifth, as G. John Ikenberry has argued, China faces an international order that is fundamentally different from those that every past rising power has confronted. China does not just confront an order upheld by a single dominant power; it faces a system that is open, integrated, rules based, and adaptable. Even with its imperfections, the current international system has wide and deep political foundations. Institutions like the World Bank and the International Monetary Fund were set up in anticipation of events such as China's rapid rise. Rather than being designed with static voting shares among members, governance is based on economic shares that are calculated by the relative weight of each economy, thus giving growing countries opportunities to gain a greater institutional voice. And in instances where China has decided to pursue a portfolio approach of expanding its shares in existing institutions and at the same time launching rival organizations of its own, such as the New Development Bank and the Asian Infrastructure Investment Bank, the international system has largely adapted to, rather than rebuked, China's initiative. These types of features give rising powers such as China ways of gaining influence without having to enter into volcanic struggles with the United States to do so.[5]

Thus, plenty of strong reasons indicate one should resist being seduced by big theoretical arguments about inevitability of conflict. Such arguments do more to conceal than clarify the character of the bilateral relationship. Leaders in the United States and China will need to look beyond such mechanical explanations of inevitable outcomes if they are to find ways to coexist, not out of amity or goodwill, but rather based on a clear-eyed recognition of each side's requirements for achieving its national ambitions.

Limiting Areas of Potential Conflict

Limiting the risk of potential conflict will require leaders in both countries to recommit to approaching the relationship as the matter-of-fact dealings of two great powers each committed to living peaceably alongside the other, as opposed to emotional contests for supremacy. Both sides will need to invest in efforts to build boundaries around issues with the greatest potential to trigger great power conflict.

Three primary risks could tip the United States and China into conflict: (1) Chinese actions that implicate the credibility of U.S. security commitments, including Taiwan, the Philippines, Japan, and the Korean Peninsula; (2) risk of collision resulting from increasingly frequent close-in military encounters between U.S. and Chinese forces; and (3) accelerating competition in new domains where rules of the road are underdeveloped or nonexistent, for example space, cyber, and autonomous weapons systems that use artificial intelligence technologies.

The starting point of a sustained effort to build boundaries around areas of potential conflict is to identify clearly what each side wants, and whether it is possible to reconcile one side's goals with the minimum requirements of the other.

In the first basket of issues—the tension between China's territorial claims and America's security commitments—there is very little overlap between U.S. requirements and Chinese objectives. At the most fundamental level, the United States wants to deter coercive attempts to resolve territorial disputes, and China wants freedom of action to employ all available tools to resolve disputes in its favor. More specifically, the United States wants to ensure that any resolution of differences over Taiwan is achieved peacefully and in a manner that reflects the free will of the Taiwan people. A similar logic applies to resolving China's contested territorial claims in the South and East China Seas. On those issues, the United States does not take a position on the underlying disputes or the ultimate disposition of any resolution but insists that they be resolved peacefully and in a manner consistent with international law. The objective, therefore, is to deter China from pursuing coercive outcomes to disputes.[6]

China, on the other hand, believes that its claims over Taiwan, in the South China Sea, and in the East China Sea are long-standing and legitimate. Beijing does not consider its pursuit of control of its claimed territories as a rebellion against the norm of sovereignty and its accompanying prohibition on territorial aggression, because

Beijing believes that the territory in question belongs to China. Communist Party leaders feel duty bound to establish control over these territories as part of their efforts to rejuvenate the country by making it whole again. Restoring territorial integrity was one of the founding promises of the Communist Party a century ago. As China moves toward the centenary of the People's Republic of China in 2049, China's leaders will likely look for ways to demonstrate directional progress, if not success, in moving these various disputes closer to resolution on China's preferred terms.

The rub is that any Chinese effort to threaten or use force to compel resolution of territorial disputes with Taiwan, the Philippines, or Japan could implicate the credibility of America's security commitments. If the United States failed to come to the common defense of its allies and security partners, it would destroy the credibility of America's security commitments, not just in Asia but around the world.

Aware of this broader American strategic imperative, Beijing to date has not directly tested America's commitments to the common defense of its allies and Taiwan. Many American analysts worry that as China's relative military capabilities expand and its capacity for localized military superiority grows, Beijing may become more risk tolerant. I fear this scenario less than others, simply because any decision to employ force to seize territory contested with an American ally or Taiwan would be a high-stakes gamble for the Chinese Communist Party. Beijing knows that absolute success is not an available option if the United States intervenes, and anything short of absolute success could invite the demise of the CCP. The Chinese are under no illusions about their ability to prevail over the U.S. military in a state of direct and outright hostilities. Institutions such as the CCP, whose topmost goal is survival, rarely take gambles when the outcome implicates their continued existence.

Even so, there is no margin for complacency in dealing with these challenges. U.S. leaders will need to remain direct and unambiguous in their dealings with Chinese counterparts in underscoring America's vital national interests in upholding the credibility of its alliance commitments, and also strengthening its deterrent capacity, as well as those of its security partners.

A goal of American strategy should be to develop a dense web of integrated security partnerships with and among American partners throughout Asia. The more that regional navies and coast guards become interoperable, the less space China will have to exert control over contested waters. Part of this effort will involve the United States making available enhanced capabilities to its security partners (for example, surveillance drones, enhanced imagery information sharing in key geographic areas, sea mines, land-based antiship missiles, fast-attack missile boats, and mobile air defenses).[7] All these weapons systems are inherently defensive; none of them are cost prohibitive.

Responding to Chinese "Salami Slicing" Tactics

While the cumulative weight of the aforementioned lines of effort would likely be enough to deter China from initiating a full-scale military campaign to seize control of contested territory, it may not be enough to deter China from pursuing incremental steps (that is, "salami slicing") in pursuit of its longer-term objectives. Admiral (Ret.) Michael McDevitt describes this Chinese approach as taking "small, incremental steps that are not likely to provoke a military response . . . but over time gradually change the status quo regarding disputed claims in its favor."[8] Beijing has shown a preference in its statecraft in recent decades for pursuing incremental gains that can be calibrated based on the external response. The most famous recent example of Chinese "salami slicing" was its construction of seven artificial features in the South China Sea.

The United States confronted a similar dilemma during the Cold War. During the 1950s, the Soviets were pushing their military capabilities outward in various parts of the world, a dynamic that greatly frustrated many in Washington at the time. Reflecting on that moment, Richard Nixon stated in 1954, "Rather than let the Communists nibble us to death all over the world in little wars we would rely in the future primarily on our massive mobile retaliatory power."[9] Such threats of massive retaliation were not credible with the Soviets then, and they would not be with China now. The Chinese know that democratic societies like the United States are cautious about initiating conflicts that could incur significant losses, as war with China surely would.[10]

Short of being prepared to escalate to direct military conflict in the face of incremental Chinese actions, it has been—and will remain—difficult for the United States to deter all such Chinese boundary pushing. The objective, therefore, is not to strive for 100 percent deterrence and then threaten a nuclear exchange if that standard is not met. Rather, it is to find ways to demonstrate credibly that the costs China incurs over time will exceed the benefits. Making such a case requires direct diplomacy with Beijing, both to elicit insight into the intended objective of China's actions and to ensure Beijing accurately interprets the full weight and intent of the U.S. response. A credible U.S. response also requires visible demonstrations of support for the aggrieved party. Depending on the circumstance, the situation may require a proportionally punitive response against China (for example, economic sanctions), as well as condemnation of the action by as large a chorus as the United States and others are able to muster.

One example of such an approach was America's response to China's sudden declaration of an air defense identification zone (ADIZ) in the East China Sea in November 2013 that overlapped the existing operational ADIZ being administered by the governing authorities of Japan, South Korea, and Taiwan. The United States responded on the same day with a joint statement from the secretaries of state and defense condemning the announcement and expressing solidarity with its alliance partners. Other countries followed suit. Shortly thereafter, the United States sent two B-52 bombers from Guam to fly through the ADIZ, thus demonstrating that China's announcement would not alter America's force posture. The next month, then–Vice President Biden traveled to Seoul and Tokyo, where he used China's action as a backdrop for strengthening alliance coordination in safeguarding regional security. Biden also traveled to Beijing, where he delivered a direct message to China's leadership about America's opposition to Beijing's announcement, and America's intolerance of any unilateral Chinese attempts to strengthen control over features in the East China Sea. Three years later, a Chinese official from the central office for foreign affairs acknowledged to me, during a candid one-on-one discussion on maritime issues on the margins of a lunch for national security advisor Susan Rice with then–state councilor Yang Jiechi, that Beijing had "miscalculated" on its ADIZ declaration.[11] To date, Beijing has not declared any other ADIZs in contested spaces and has not sought to use the ADIZ to impede lawful operations of U.S. military aircraft in the East China Sea.

A narrow interpretation of those events would suggest that China took a bold move and was not forced to roll it back. A broader review of the episode would conclude that China's sudden announcement undermined trust with Seoul and Tokyo, provided a pretext for the United States to involve itself more visibly in regional security affairs, led to a strengthening of America's security relations with South Korea and Japan, raised regional awareness of Beijing's imperious approach to regional security, and visibly highlighted the impotence of Beijing's ability to curtail lawful American military activities. The cost that Beijing incurred for its ADIZ announcement exceeded the benefit it accrued.

The South China Sea

A less effective American response to Chinese boundary testing was the response to Beijing's construction of seven artificial islands in the South China Sea. Beijing compensated for its numerical inferiority in the South China Sea—it occupies only 27 of the 93 outposts within its nine-dash line claim in the South China Sea—by significantly enhancing the size and force projection capabilities of each of its occupied features. From 2013 to 2016, China added around 3,200 acres of land to its occupied outposts, allowing for the construction of airstrips, military barracks, sensor towers, and missile systems on several of its features.[12] Through its land reclamation, as well as its expanding naval and air presence, China in a brief period went from an inferior position to one of military strength relative to other claimants in the South China Sea. In response, the United States and others sought to raise the reputational costs to China of altering the status quo and seemingly seeking to strengthen its capacity to control contested waters and vital waterways. The Philippines pursued a legal strategy to undermine China's claims through the International Tribunal for the Law of the Sea. Washington maintained a steady military presence in the South China Sea and resumed freedom-of-navigation operations to assert its legal rights to unimpeded operations there. Even so, a perception solidified throughout the region that China was on the march and the United States was either unable or unwilling to obstruct it.

Practically speaking, the situation in the South China Sea stands at a stalemate, with China unable to push the United States out without risking conflict, and the United States unable to push China off its reclaimed features without risking conflict. Nevertheless, perceptually the United States failed to impose costs on China that exceeded its perceived strategic benefits.

Taiwan

While much of the logic of deterrence similarly applies to America's approach to Taiwan, there are several important qualifications. First, the U.S. strategic objective is to preserve the status quo until leaders on both sides of the Taiwan Strait are able to identify a peaceful solution to differences. The more the United States becomes partisan in support of either Taiwan independence or unification, the more hostility its actions will engender, and the less influence it will wield over cross-Strait developments.

Second, America's natural sympathies lie with the people of Taiwan. The people of Taiwan have built a vibrant democracy and a thriving economy even as they have lived under constant pressure from Beijing. At the same time, not every international problem has an American solution. Taiwan is a case in point.

The United States will need to be prepared to exercise its leverage with both Beijing and Taipei, as it has done before, to keep open the path to a peaceful solution. This will require the United States to be prepared to stand in the way of the two paths that could trigger hostilities involving the United States: coerced unification and contested de jure independence. America's strategy should be to foreclose attempts by either side to pursue efforts that could trigger conflict. For more than forty years, American policy has been based on the tenet that the longer the situation remains peaceful, the greater the possibility that wisdom will ultimately prevail and leaders on both sides of the Taiwan Strait will identify a peaceful solution that allows the people of Taiwan to enjoy the peace and prosperity they deserve.

It is also worth recalling the formidable risks for Beijing of attempting to impose an outcome on Taiwan through force. All previous Chinese attempts to coerce Taiwan through threat or use of force, dating back to the Chinese shelling of offshore islands in the 1950s through its missile exercises against Taiwan on the eve of its 1996 elections, have weakened, rather than strengthened, Beijing's influence on Taiwan. Beijing faces uncertain prospects of being able to prevail militarily, particularly if the United States intervenes. It also is aware of the damage to China's regional and global aspirations and image that would result from any assault on Taiwan. Additionally, Beijing's challenges in pacifying the situation in Hong

Kong, a geographically contiguous area with a much smaller population and a lesser capacity for self-defense, has only reinforced the challenge China would confront in seeking to assert control over Taiwan. Such an outcome would be anything but assured.

Even so, it is vital for the United States to retain a credible military deterrent. If Beijing initiates hostilities toward Taiwan, the United States must be prepared to come to Taiwan's defense. While American force readiness is a critical element of deterrence, so too is Taiwan's consistent investments in its own defense, including adopting asymmetric and innovative approaches that augment Taiwan's geographic advantages. A much larger element, though, is for the people of Taiwan to forge a more pragmatic political consensus around ways to strengthen their society and improve their economic competitiveness. The more successful Taiwan becomes, the less vulnerable to Chinese predation it will be.

The Korean Peninsula

The last battleground of direct U.S.-China conflict was the Korean Peninsula. Although tensions remain elevated there now owing to North Korea's ongoing development of nuclear weapons and missile delivery systems, the likelihood of a conflict that could draw U.S. and PRC forces into direct conflict remains low. Both Washington and Beijing have a much clearer understanding of each other's strategic requirements on the Korean Peninsula now relative to 1950, and both sides maintain more robust and direct channels to register concerns and clarify intentions. Additionally, given the impossibility for the United States of mitigating the potential devastation of Seoul and surrounding areas from any hostilities with North Korea, the likelihood of a U.S.-initiated strike against North Korea that could compel a Chinese military response is very low. Nevertheless, the risk is not zero. There remains a stubborn possibility of North Korean boundary testing that could trigger an escalation to conflict. As such, it will remain imperative for Washington and Beijing to sustain direct and authoritative communication on North Korea.[13]

In sum, in the cases of the South and East China Seas and Taiwan, the United States' objective is defensive and defensible. The United States seeks to uphold the status quo, and China is attempting to alter it. Prudence dictates that in the face of China's rapid growth in military capabilities, the United States and its partners have a responsibility to maintain defensive capabilities at sufficient levels so as to make it prohibitively risky for any Chinese leaders to attempt to seize contested territory by force. Given the conflicting priorities between the United States and China in each of these scenarios, for the foreseeable future a real possibility of metal-on-metal friction remains. The more that Washington and Beijing can agree on common rules of the road for managing such frictions before they occur, the lower the likelihood that they could escalate rapidly to conflict.

Risk Management

Although neither side views conflict as being in its interest, the physics of frequent close-in military operations make such a scenario a live possibility. To reduce risk of such an outcome, both sides should draw lessons from the Cold War.

Even at the zenith of Cold War competition, and sometimes because of it, American and Soviet leaders demonstrated alacrity and energy in reducing risks of accidental and unplanned hostilities. Influenced by a shared acceptance of the concept of mutually assured destruction, leaders in both capitals showed statesmanship in lowering nuclear risks, including the 1963 Partial Test Ban Treaty, the 1967 treaty prohibiting testing of nuclear weapons in outer space, the 1970 Treaty on Non-Proliferation of Nuclear Weapons (NPT), the 1972 Strategic Arms Limitation Talks agreement, the 1972 Biological Weapons Convention and Anti-Ballistic Missile

Treaty, the Intermediate-Range Nuclear Forces Treaty (INF) in 1987, and the Strategic Arms Reduction Treaties (START I and START II) signed between 1991 and 1993. They also conducted high-stakes horse trading around removing nuclear warheads from Cuba and Turkey, respectively, during the Cuban Missile Crisis of 1962.

Similar efforts extended beyond nuclear risk reduction. President John F. Kennedy and First Secretary Nikita Khrushchev established a leader-level hotline to mitigate risk of catastrophic miscalculations. In a sad twist of history, the assassination of Kennedy served as the impetus for the first use of the hotline. The two governments also established the Incidents at Sea Agreement in 1972 to govern rules of engagement at sea and in the air, as well as the Conventional Forces in Europe treaty to determine acceptable ranges of deployments of military hardware like tanks and aircraft.

Efforts between Washington and Beijing to reduce risk today, by comparison, are quite immature. The recent high point of such efforts was the joint announcement in 2015 of two agreements, the first to establish shared rules of behavior for surface and air encounters between U.S. and Chinese military platforms, and the second to notify each other about major military activities. A subsequent third agreement established protocols for crisis communications between both countries' respective military headquarters. These agreements were envisioned by Obama and Xi at the time as building blocks for further agreements to limit risk of unintended incidents; however, the two governments have not made progress in negotiating new annexes since these initial agreements were inked.

Part of the tension in making further progress on risk reduction is that both sides hold different priorities. The United States wants to preserve unimpeded military operations anywhere that international law allows, whereas China wants to push American military operations farther from its shores and to gain greater transparency on such activities. Therefore Chinese officials prioritize notifications of military exercises and missile tests, and American officials focus on ensuring that Chinese military operators adhere to internationally accepted protocols when operating near American platforms.

Another obstacle to progress on risk reduction is that the Pacific has no effective lines of demarcation, as there were in Central Europe during the Cold War. During the Cold War, each side recognized clear geographic boundaries that came to be known as the Iron Curtain. Now, U.S. and Chinese naval and air platforms intermingle on a daily basis throughout maritime Asia; the frequency of interaction is rising as both countries field more—and more capable—assets that operate in close proximity.

Finally, neither military sees profit in acting as the ardent suitor for agreements that would constrain their activities. Left to their own devices, neither military would willingly pursue further risk reduction measures that would limit their freedom of maneuver. As a consequence, if they are to achieve any progress, both militaries will need to be directed by their national leaders to prioritize risk reduction.

One way to restart progress on risk reduction initiatives would be for both leaders to signal their expectation that they will use leader-level meetings as action-forcing events to advance risk reduction initiatives, much as U.S. and Soviet leaders did during the Cold War. It would also behoove the United States to encourage other regional countries similarly to prioritize the establishment of military risk reduction protocols in their own leader-level diplomacy with China. The more that international expectations are set for how China conducts itself as a major naval and air power, the higher the likelihood of movement toward consistently safe and professional conduct.

New Domains of Military Competition

At the height of Cold War tensions in the 1960s and 1970s, the United States, the Soviet Union, and other countries spent billions

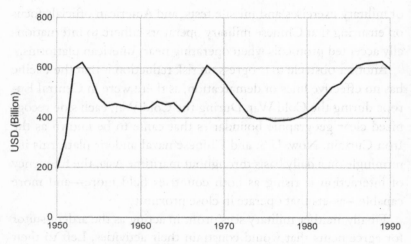

U.S. nominal historic defense spending, 1950–1990
Data from U.S. Office of Management and Budget

of dollars developing new weapons capabilities. The pace of research, development, and deployment often outran efforts to establish norms and rules of the road that could lessen the security dilemma created by the introduction of these new capabilities.

We may be living today through an analogous period of rapid advancement in military capabilities and transformation in the conduct of warfare. The United States, China, Russia, and others are pouring billions of dollars into new technologies, including offensive cyber capabilities, AI-enhanced weapons systems, hypersonic glide vehicles, nuclear force modernization, and offensive capabilities in space. As the arms control expert and former diplomat Thomas Countryman and others have warned, failing to get in front of dangers resulting from these new weapons capabilities now could heighten countries' senses of vulnerability and lead to intensifying efforts to develop countermeasures.[14]

China has been at the leading edge of many of these recent technological developments. It is rapidly modernizing its strategic nuclear forces. It is developing new capabilities to launch nuclear-tipped intercontinental missiles from land, sea, and air (the nuclear triad). It has pushed forward a dramatic expansion of its medium- and intermediate-range ballistic and cruise missile capabilities. China is developing hypersonic glide vehicles that reportedly travel more than five times the speed of sound and are capable of maneuvering to avoid detection. China's (and Russia's) advances in this domain have prompted the Pentagon's undersecretary of defense for research and engineering to warn that the United States lacks defenses against such systems and would not be able to counter them if they were employed.[15] Beijing has also invested significantly in developing antisatellite systems, including jammers, kinetic kill systems, lasers, and on-orbit systems. China is actively developing robust offensive cyberattack capabilities that threaten America's military and critical infrastructure systems.[16] Beijing has also invested in other technologies, such as life sciences and quantum computing, although the time horizon for realizing many of those capabilities remains farther off.

China's massive investments often focus on developing capabilities that target American vulnerabilities. Beijing is improving its ability to hold the continental United States at risk (nuclear and offensive cyber capabilities), threaten the safety of U.S. forces operating in the western Pacific (new cruise, ballistic, and hypersonic missiles), and make vulnerable America's access to space-derived satellite data on which its national and economic security depends (antisatellite systems). China is also pushing forward aggressively in developing autonomous and AI-enhanced weaponry, which holds the potential to rapidly accelerate the velocity and lethality of warfighting. Cumulatively, these technological advancements generate acute national security threats that the United States has grown unaccustomed to confronting in the post–Cold War era.

According to my many conversations about these developments with Chinese officials, though, from Beijing's perspective China

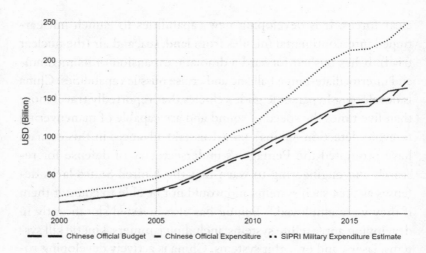

China's military spending
Data from Stockholm International Peace Research Institute,
Ministry of National Defense, National Bureau of Statistics

remains relatively more vulnerable to American capabilities and is investing in capabilities to neutralize American advantages. Beijing believes it must continually lean forward in developing countermeasures to America's military superiority to preserve strategic stability with the United States, which Chinese officials define as a state of mutual vulnerability. Otherwise, according to their logic, Beijing risks falling into a scenario whereby the United States establishes "absolute security" against Chinese military capabilities, at which point it could coerce China into bending to its will because the risks and costs of defying American demands would become too high to tolerate.

In other words, the United States and China are locked in a classic security dilemma. Both sides feel vulnerable, each believes it is responding to actions of the other, and neither feels comfortable pulling back the throttle on its national weapons development programs because each side fears that the other is a revisionist and power-maximizing actor. There are no easy trade-offs or silver-bullet solutions to escape this dilemma. Rather, leaders in both countries will need to direct their national security teams to work with their counterparts to develop rules of the road for emerging technologies and, in the process, lower the risk of great power conflict.

Norm Building

Much as mutual fear of catastrophic scenarios motivated Washington and Moscow during the Cold War, so too should it prompt Washington and Beijing now to explore avenues for risk reduction. From an American perspective, the objective should be to enlist China's participation in rule making and then work to bind Chinese behavior to the rules that are set. Such efforts have historical precedents. During the Cold War, the United States and the Soviet Union stood at the core of efforts to develop limitations around issues such as appropriate uses of chemical weapons and then worked outward to attract others to join in supporting and ratifying understandings reached between them, ultimately resulting in the Chemical Weapons Convention.

As the two dominant actors today, the United States and China will jointly need to accept responsibility for standing at the core of efforts to develop rules of the road around emerging technologies and then pursuing an inkblot approach of steadily involving more parties in developing a normative framework. Both will need to accept the reality that the only way to realize international norms of acceptable behavior in emerging military technologies will be through the active participation and support of the United States and China.

This process will present challenges for the United States. The United States can ill afford to project a G2 vision of the world wherein Washington and Beijing decide among themselves and then dictate terms to allies and partners based on understandings reached between the two powers. Such a perception would be corrosive to America's alliances and security partnerships. To limit risk of such a perception emerging, the United States will need to exhibit diplomatic dexterity, both in consulting with allies and partners about approaches to Beijing and in maintaining maximal transparency with them about the status of efforts with Beijing to negotiate understandings. The United States has done this before. Though on a less sensitive scale, Washington performed this dance between Beijing and its allies during negotiations leading up to the closure of the Paris climate accord in 2016.

In developing rules of the road for emerging technologies, both countries should be guided by pragmatism and determination to make progress where possible. The goal should be to take more and more problems off the table over time, rather than hold out for some grand bargain that may never arrive. Success in reducing risk in small areas can generate momentum toward more ambitious risk reduction efforts in the future. Initial steps that both countries could feasibly take at little cost to either side could include the development of a bilateral prelaunch missile notification regime for missiles that extend beyond a certain range; the establishment of a direct link between the U.S. Nuclear Risk Reduction Center and its Chinese counterpart; and a shared commitment to refrain from activities in space that create orbital debris.[17]

Such initial steps could generate mutual confidence to address larger challenges, such as developing a norm against using kinetic antisatellite weapons in outer space or agreeing that nuclear early warning and launch decisions must remain under direct human control and not be activated by artificial intelligence and machine learning algorithms. Both sides could also conceivably agree on out-of-bounds targets for cyberattacks, for example hospitals, critical infrastructure, and so on. Such efforts would build on previous discussions about these topics toward the end of the Obama administration.[18]

Additional Lines of Effort

The United States will have to make two other significant adjustments in its approach to the region to better align its capabilities with its ambitions.

First, as the former Trump administration defense planner Elbridge Colby has written, the United States needs to accept that its run of untrammeled military superiority in Asia is over.[19] No levers are available to the United States to turn back the clock to the period of military primacy it enjoyed in Asia for decades.

Over time, America's force posture will need to adapt to the new reality that it can no longer act with impunity in the region. This will require U.S. doctrine to shift from a specific focus on territorial defense to a broader posture of deterring aggression through a credible ability to impose massive costs on potential aggressors, though not necessarily at the geographic point of attack.[20]

Second, the United States needs to reconceptualize how it conducts military operations in the face of China's growing military capabilities. Although China's military power falls off rapidly with distance, it remains potent within its near periphery. To maintain the ability to deter Chinese threats or use of force against American allies and security partners in China's near periphery, the United States will need to become more vigilant about concentrating power for dealing with China, and more creative about updating its defense concepts for doing so.

To concentrate military power for dealing with China, the United States will need to wean itself off its habit of acting as a global policeman, deploying forces to address challenges in regions of the world that do not implicate America's vital interests. As noble as American efforts have been in recent decades to shield vulnerable populations from predation and promote freedom and human progress, those efforts have come at considerable expense, sapped American strength, and lost the support of the American public. It is no coincidence that the last three American presidential candidates to win election have been the ones who vowed to end wars and refocus on problems at home.

In that vein, one could do worse than to resurrect the Powell Doctrine before sending American soldiers into harm's way. As chairman of the Joint Chiefs of Staff, General Colin Powell argued that seven questions needed to be answered affirmatively before he would support American armed intervention: (1) Is a vital national security interest threatened? (2) Does the United States have a clear and attainable objective? (3) Have the risks and costs been fully and credibly analyzed? (4) Have all other nonviolent options been fully exhausted? (5) Is there a credible exit strategy to conflict? (6) Is the action supported by the U.S. citizenry? (7) Does the United States have genuine and broad international support? The discipline embedded in this doctrine would help the United States avoid entering costly future quagmires and limit the risk of America getting sucked farther into the Middle East.

At the same time, the United States will also need to reimagine how it employs force in crisis scenarios with China. As the defense expert Christian Brose has observed, "Since the end of the Cold War, the United States' approach to projecting military force against regional powers has rested on a series of assumptions about how conflict will unfold. The U.S. military assumes that its forces will be able to move unimpeded into forward positions and that it will be able to commence hostilities at a time of its choosing. It assumes that its forces will operate in permissive environments—that adversaries will be unable to contest its freedom of movement in any domain. It assumes that any quantitative advantage that an adversary may possess will be overcome by its own superior ability to evade detection, penetrate enemy defenses, and strike targets."[21] None of those assumptions hold in a military scenario involving China. Instead, China is developing and fielding large numbers of multi-million-dollar platforms to destroy America's multi-billion-dollar platforms.

To counter this evolving challenge, the military expert Michael O'Hanlon argues that the United States should deploy "a plethora of relatively small, fast, precise, inexpensive, autonomous weapons [that] could threaten large exposed objects such as ships, planes, ports, and rail lines—to say nothing of other fixed infrastructure, such as fiber-optic cables, electricity-generating equipment and transmission lines, bridges and tunnels, and other infrastructure of crucial importance to modern militaries on the move."[22] Relying on large numbers of smaller autonomous systems would generate vast networks that China would need to defend against, and also reduce America's current vulnerabilities to single points of failure (for example, if an aircraft carrier or command ship is destroyed). Aircraft carriers and large capital ships will retain their role in projecting presence, reassurance, and raising the threshold for China to decide to launch military operations against an American security partner, but such vessels will make up a lesser element of American operational planning in wartime contingencies.

Such a shift in doctrinal thinking would make U.S. forces more denial oriented by raising risks to Chinese forces of entering "kill zones" off China's shores. It would also reduce the risk of large-scale losses. To make it possible to field such a lethal, agile, and ready force, though, the United States will also need to make its bases and operating locations in Asia more resilient and geographically dispersed, and not dependent on a small number of fixed-hub bases that fall within China's missile envelope and would likely be neutralized by Chinese strikes at the outset of hostilities.[23]

Conclusion

An honest assessment of the present disposition of military forces in the region makes clear that the United States will need to align its capabilities with its ambitions in an era of growing fiscal constraints. At the same time, Washington and Beijing will also need to invigorate efforts to identify how best to protect their own vital interests without impinging on each other's in the process. This task will be difficult, but not impossible, so long as leaders in both countries resist impulses toward "king of the hill" competition and instead work toward developing a new equilibrium for the relationship that allows them to coexist within a state of heightened competition.

Leading American and Asian strategists, including Lee Kuan Yew, Henry Kissinger, Brent Scowcroft, Barack Obama, George Kennan, and many others, have all coalesced around a judgment that intensifying competition between the United States and China would be inevitable, but conflict would not. Their predictions have proved prescient up to now. Heightened competition and absence of direct military conflict remain the most likely foreseeable scenario for the U.S.-China relationship today. It falls to future generations of American and Chinese leaders and policy makers to ensure that this remains the case going forward.

Navigating Great Power Relations

The United States naturally has common interests with the European Union, India, and Japan in wanting China to forgo bullying behavior while accepting greater responsibilities for addressing global challenges. This broad alignment of objectives should incentivize America to explore ways to work in common cause with these powers to push China's rise into a tolerable trajectory. Achieving greater coordination with other major powers will require the United States to keep its focus on areas where interests naturally align, accepting that other major powers will be less willing to push back on Chinese behavior in certain areas. Washington will also need to exercise discipline in not allowing lesser bilateral irritants to obstruct cooperation on the topmost strategic challenge: managing China's rise. In the case of Russia, the United States' objective should be to slow the pace of convergence between Beijing and Moscow, trusting that over time divergences in both countries' worldviews and strategic objectives will bring the relationship back to a more historically normal equilibrium. As long as the United States remains capable of working with its friends productively to manage China's rise, Washington will be able to preserve a favorable balance of power in the international system.

Context

Despite their sharp ideological differences in the early 1970s, the United States and China were originally brought together in service of great power competition: limiting the Soviet Union's expansion of influence. In the decades that followed, the United States preserved its privileged position in the triangular relationship between Washington, Beijing, and Moscow, in the sense of maintaining the best relationship with the other two. Even when Washington encountered friction with China and Russia, it could still rely on its preponderant position in the international system to keep Beijing and Moscow invested in pursuing generally constructive, or at a minimum nonhostile, relations.

That is no longer the case. Today, China occupies the central position in the triangular relationship. Relations between Moscow and Beijing have strengthened as America's relations with both have grown antagonistic. This diminution of America's place has led to a widely held sense that China and Russia are making strides, reshaping the world to suit their interests at America's expense. Reams of reports now paint a picture of how China and Russia are working to fracture Europe, gain advantage in the Middle East, transform Africa, carve up Central Asia, and make inroads in Latin America.

U.S. policy makers today are unaccustomed to feeling disadvantaged on the world stage. But this moment is not the first when the United States has encountered a sense of vulnerability. For much of the country's history, the United States has felt vulnerable to external threats of one form or another. The unipolar moment that lasted from the end of the Cold War until the global financial crisis of 2008 was very much the exception.

The most recent analogy to our current moment may be the 1960s. As in the present, the United States at that time was coming off a period of unrivaled dominance. In the preceding decade, it had enjoyed global military, economic, and diplomatic superiority; Europe and Japan were devastated, China was in the midst of a civil war, and Russia was busy rebuilding itself.

Then, over a short period, the Soviet Union shocked the United States back into competition. Moscow launched the *Sputnik* rocket into orbit, began actively tightening its grip over countries behind the Iron Curtain, and seemed to be achieving gains in spreading and solidifying its ideology in regions ranging from Latin America to Africa and Asia.

As but one example illustrating the anxieties that were being induced at the time, the *New York Times* ran an editorial on March 1, 1964, about America's foreign policy. In it, the editorial board wrote:

> We like the world—our world—and cling to it with all our strength, but the world has been slipping out of our grasp. There is what Prof. Denis Brogan long ago called "the illusion of American omnipotence," and since we are not all-powerful and cannot mold the world in our image, there is frustration, anger, criticism of the Government, a search for scapegoats. Some find their answers in blaming Communism, yet no major Western power and no region outside the Communist bloc— Latin America, Africa, the Middle East, Asia—sees the Communist menace in American terms.[1]

The United States finds itself in a similar moment yet again. The recent shift in the global distribution of power has tapped deep anxieties about America losing its grip on the world and becoming more vulnerable as a result. COVID-19 and its aftereffects have yet again shattered the illusion of American omnipotence. This humility-inducing era, in turn, has fueled the emergence of a cottage industry of analysts seeking to define the current transformation of the international system.

For example, Ian Bremmer, founder of the Eurasia Group, has

coined the concept of a "G-zero world," meaning that as the United States turns inward, there is no longer any single country or group of countries with the capacity and the will to lead the international system.[2] Neoconservatives such as the Brookings scholar Robert Kagan have warned that American retreat from global leadership will lead to a "return of the jungle" mentality in the international system, where the strong do what they will, the weak do what they must, and left unchecked, illiberalism and chaos will reemerge as defining features of international relations.[3] Assertive realists like John Bolton have argued that the United States must use its muscle to turn back the clock to the period of American primacy in the global system. In their telling, the central goal of U.S. grand strategy must be to "prevail" over China and other rivals.[4] The U.S. government has defined the current moment as a return of great power competition and has warned that "China and Russia want to shape a world consistent with their authoritarian model—gaining veto authority over other nations' economic, diplomatic, and security decisions."[5]

While each of these analyses is thought-provoking, they all miss the mark in diagnosing the transformation taking place in the international system. The overarching story of this period is not the reemergence of universalistic ideological struggle, or of some Hobbesian world, or of a leadership vacuum. Authoritarianism is not an ideology but a form of governance,[6] and China's governance model holds little attraction outside its borders, foremost among those who understand it best, the people of Hong Kong and Taiwan. At the same time, even as the United States and others are stepping back, a network of civic organizations, corporations, and philanthropic leaders are stepping forward. Armed with data and equipped with abundant resources, organizations like the Gates Foundation and Médecins Sans Frontières are working to fill gaps, eradicate diseases, improve access to education, and elevate quality-of-life metrics on every continent. As but one example, when President

Trump announced on April 15, 2020, that the United States would withhold funds from the World Health Organization out of pique that the WHO seemed unduly sympathetic to China's viewpoints on COVID-19, Bill Gates responded the next day by donating the equivalent of the U.S. withholding in dues through the Gates Foundation.

Viewed broadly, there has never been a better time to be alive. As the Brookings scholar Homi Kharas and Kristofer Hamel from World Data Lab have documented, for the first time since agriculture-based civilization began ten thousand years ago, the majority of humankind is no longer poor or vulnerable to falling into poverty. Today, just over 50 percent of the world population, or some 3.8 billion people, has reached the middle class or moved beyond it to affluence.[7]

The world also is largely free of the risk of deliberate and direct great power conflict. As the Brookings scholar Michael O'Hanlon has argued, "Strong American-led alliances, conventional and nuclear deterrence, and economic interdependence all militate strongly against any conscious decision by a [great power] adversary to initiate large-scale war."[8] And even as several of the world's leading democracies have seen their luster dim amid troubling instances of democratic backsliding, more people now live in democracies than at any other point in history, thanks largely to the consolidation of democracy across parts of Asia and Africa.[9] So, even amid America's inward turn and its shrinking efforts to exercise global leadership, irrefutable indicators still point to progress in improving the human condition.

If this time has a defining feature, it would be the widening gap in overall national power of the United States and China from the rest of the pack, and the implications of these two major powers surging ahead for regional and global stability. Even as competition between the United States and China is intensifying, both countries are simultaneously expanding the distance between themselves and every other country in economic size, pace of innovation, defense spending, and overall national power.

Other major powers in the international system will continue to exercise significant influence, foremost among them the European Union, Russia, India, and Japan. Each of these has a major population and substantial economic weight or military heft, but none have all.[10] This puts them a big step behind the United States and China, with little likelihood of closing the gap anytime soon. Below these major powers are also significant regional powers. These include Iran in the Middle East, Nigeria and South Africa in Africa, and Brazil and Mexico in Latin America. This new configuration will involve constant tension in creating and sustaining durable regional balances of power. It will require major powers to gain cooperation and support of regional and lesser powers. But most of all, it will depend on relations among the major powers.

Leaders and leading thinkers in Beijing readily acknowledge that China enters this competition with the United States from a deficit. China lacks the global network of friends and allies that the United States has cultivated over decades. That is why strategists such as the Tsinghua University professor Yan Xuetong have argued, for example, that "to shape a friendly international environment for its rise, Beijing needs to develop more high-quality diplomatic and military relationships than Washington. . . . The core of competition will be to see who has more high-quality friends."[11]

Particularly as U.S.-China competition has intensified in recent years, Beijing has sought with varying degrees of success to ameliorate points of friction in its relationships with other major powers, including Japan, India, and the European Union. Beijing recognizes its need to cultivate closer relations with other major powers to advance its broader foreign policy goals—reclaiming what it views as its rightful historical place as the central power in Asia and a great power globally.

At the same time, China's leaders are acutely sensitive to the fact that China relies more on the outside world for its progress than at any time in its millennial history. Given both its geostrategic ambitions and its technological and natural resource deficits, China requires imports from abroad to sustain its population and support its continued economic expansion. As India's former national security advisor Shivshankar Menon has observed, "It is China's dependence on the world for energy, commodities, technology, and markets that drives her to consolidate Eurasia and attempt to transform herself into a maritime power."[12]

U.S. Objectives in Great Power Relationships

The United States does not need to defeat China or thwart its rise. It is not engaged in a universalistic ideological struggle with China because Beijing does not have the capacity to inspire or compel others to adopt its political model. The goal is not to push China back within its borders or to starve it of productive relations with other powers, particularly since such outcomes are not available to the United States. Rather, America's foremost objectives in the context of great power relations are to (1) increase pressure on Beijing to forgo bullying behavior, (2) constrain the spread of malign aspects of China's governance system, and (3) urge Beijing to accept greater burdens in global governance commensurate with its growing leadership role in the international system.

Apart from Russia, all the other major powers share similar objectives with the United States. The more the United States can find ways to work in lockstep with the European Union, India, and Japan to push China in this preferred direction of forgoing bullying behavior and accepting greater international responsibilities, the higher the likelihood of progress. Harnessing greater collaboration among major powers, though, will require the United States to abandon its seeming indifference to the interests and anxieties of other major powers. Instead the United States will need to regain strategic altruism, letting go of lesser irritants, taking a long-term view of its interests, and prioritizing efforts that will unlock greater coordination with the European Union, India, and Japan on influencing China's behavior.

In pursuing such coordination, Washington must bear in mind that each of these partners has its own unique goals with, and perceptions of, China. All these major powers have significant economic ties with China, and all seek a generally constructive relationship with China. As such, a consultative and flexible American approach toward coordinating actions in support of common objectives with other major powers will prove more effective than any attempt to build a bloc to counter China.

The goal of American strategy should not be to seize opportunities to denigrate China or obstruct its development, or to insist that other major powers align with the United States in opposing China. Rather, the goal should be to form patterns of coordination with other major powers in instances where interests converge. At times, this may involve joint efforts to impede Chinese actions of concern. At other times, it may call for joint efforts to seek to induce greater Chinese contributions to common challenges. Throughout, the United States should seek to cultivate closer, denser, more beneficial relations with other major powers than those powers have with China. The more closely the United States can demonstrate commonality of effort with them on China, the more leverage it will accrue for influencing Chinese behavior.

Such efforts would be strengthened by America's revitalization of its past role as the leading global convening power. Washington in the past has brought together countries for collective problem-solving that makes all countries better off, for example launching the G20 after the global financial crisis, creating the Nuclear Security Summit to limit the spread of nuclear material, and developing the Global Health Security Agenda to combat the spread of infectious diseases. As G. John Ikenberry has observed, "When other countries see the United States using its power to strengthen existing rules and institutions [or creating new ones], that power is rendered more legitimate—and U.S. authority is strengthened."[13] Such efforts should include China. Bringing China into the fold increases peer pressure on Beijing to contribute more to global public goods.

Relatedly, the United States must restore an affirmative agenda with Beijing on transnational challenges. The absence of any affirmative agenda for the relationship during the Trump administration has lowered the opportunity cost for Beijing of pursuing closer relations with Moscow. Beijing had little to lose and much to gain by edging toward Moscow.

For reasons I discuss later, Russia needs to be placed in a separate category from other major powers. The United States will need to pursue a more patient and longer-term approach for creating separation in the Sino-Russian relationship, even as it works in the short term to slow the pace of convergence between the two nations.

Build a Common Agenda with the European Union

Over the past decade, China has made significant economic and strategic inroads in Europe. It has lavished European countries with preferential trade and investment. It has persistently engaged at the leader level, as well as across a range of sectors, from sports to the arts, academics, the environment, and health research. China has emerged as the European Union's second-largest trading partner, behind only the United States. This surge of Chinese investment and engagement in Europe has fed perceptions across the continent that the future lies with China. China is widely perceived as the most important swing buyer in the global economy. Even the United Kingdom, traditionally America's closest ally, now treats China as the country with the most unrealized potential in the world. China has nurtured this perception, for example through its sweeping pronouncements of plans to link China to Europe through the Belt and Road Initiative (BRI). After being viewed warily at first, the BRI has gained greater acceptance and support on the continent, with Italy becoming the first G7 member to join in 2019.

On the diplomatic front, China has maintained steady contact with the major European powers—Germany, France, and the United Kingdom—while becoming a friend to those in need, such as Greece and Hungary. Beijing has pursued strategic investments in European ports, including the Greek port of Piraeus, as well as terminals in Belgium, Italy, Spain, and the Netherlands. It has showered money on leading high-tech companies across the continent, often offering to pay above market value for stakes in firms. It has also developed new mechanisms for engaging subsets of the continent, most notably the 17+1 mechanism, which brings together mostly southern, central, and eastern European leaders with their Chinese counterparts every year.

These Chinese actions have been guided by Beijing's identification of its interests in Europe, namely, to (1) secure legitimization as a global power; (2) profit from access to an integrated European market; (3) diversify sources of high-tech inputs into the Chinese economy as a hedge against overreliance on imports from the United States; (4) limit pressure from European countries—and especially from the European Union—on sensitive political issues; and (5) open up space between the United States and the European Union. The last objective helps Beijing lower the risk of Western countries joining forces against China, either to condemn Chinese behavior or to challenge its rise. It also helps slow down efforts by the West to promulgate new international rules and norms that do not align with Chinese interests or preferences.

Beijing has made considerable progress in advancing these objectives, both through its own actions and as a consequence of transatlantic rifts that have widened during the Trump presidency. Much as it has done with its co-optation of Laos and Cambodia within the Association of Southeast Asian Nations, China appears to have found ways to get inside the EU tent to halt collective actions against it. Greece and Hungary have become reliable defenders of Beijing, and Italy and Portugal appear to be trending toward joining them as outliers within the EU.[14]

China has also established itself as an alternative funding source for illiberal European regimes that are coming under pressure from the EU. Beijing's enabling of an illiberal shift in countries like Hungary and Romania is blemishing the democratic complexion of the EU, leading to much angst in Brussels and elsewhere about Chinese (and Russian) authoritarian influence spreading across Europe. Reports of Chinese attempts to influence media discourse in Europe, such as targeted investments and the spread of content from Chinese state media via established news outlets, have heightened these concerns.[15]

Partly as a result, growing voices in Europe are calling for a reevaluation of the EU's approach to China. This was evident, for example, in the European Commission's March 2019 report on China that characterized China for the first time as a "systemic rival."[16] One should note, though, that the same report also referred to China as a "strategic partner" and a "competitor," underscoring the difficult balance that Europe is seeking to strike.

From an American perspective, a practical strategy with Europe on China would be based on a sober evaluation of how far the European Union and individual European partners are prepared to go in pushing back on Chinese actions of concern. Broadly speaking, many European leaders still see China as both an opportunity and a threat, thus placing them on a different page from the prevailing view in Washington. Even so, there still are specific, concrete areas where strengthening coordination would serve European and American interests.

For example, European nations share an interest with the United States in upholding international maritime law. The European Union has the world's largest maritime exclusive economic zone. China's actions along its periphery, including the South China Sea, directly call into question the continuing efficacy of established rules for managing maritime issues, most notably the United Nations Convention on the Law of the Sea. The United States should work with European countries that possess sufficient naval capacity to conduct presence and freedom-of-navigation operations throughout Asia, both to foreclose any Chinese consideration of employing coercion to settle territorial disputes, and to reinforce the continuing applicability of freedom of navigation and overflight in international waters.[17] The United Kingdom and France have already taken cautious steps in this direction.[18] Such efforts should be augmented going forward.

There may also be scope for greater sharing of best practices on closing loopholes for foreign interference in national and regional elections, much as Australia recently has done. At the moment, only around half of Europe's member states fully ban foreign donations in elections.[19] European nations may also find mutual benefit to sharing best practices on establishing carefully crafted foreign investment screening procedures for inbound investments in national security-sensitive fields.

Another area of natural convergence is human rights. The United States and the EU should rediscover their voices for pushing China to implement its commitments under the Universal Declaration of Human Rights and the International Covenant on Civil and Political Rights. Relatedly, the United States and the EU also share an interest in ensuring a resilient, independent, open, and free media environment, not just in Europe but around the world. A free press provides an essential check against the spread of corruption and the normalization of coercion. Both the United States and the EU could pool resources to promote projects that seek to strengthen journalistic independence and integrity around the world.

On the economic front, American and European companies are both similarly disadvantaged by China's state-led mercantilist economic model. This should provide incentive for coordinating efforts to push China to reform its state-backed mercantilist model, including improving intellectual property protections and enforcing rules against forced technology transfer. It should also provide a basis for coordinated efforts to press China to join the World Trade Organization government procurement agreement and to support reforms to the WTO more broadly. These could include new disciplines on industrial subsidies and cross-border data flows, for example.

A transatlantic strategy on China should not focus only on countering Chinese policies, though. It must also seek to elicit more and better Chinese contributions for addressing challenges that all three actors—the EU, the United States, and China—confront. Climate change presents a ripe area for joint action. The United States and the EU should encourage and welcome China's international leadership on mitigation and adaptation efforts. At the same time, the United States and the EU should also urge China to refrain from building or financing additional coal-fired power plants through its foreign investment and aid programs, or at a minimum aggressively phase out coal-fired power stations by a certain date.

Similarly, all three actors may find space for complementary effort on development programs. All three would benefit from greater transparency about projects being undertaken and better sharing of best practices in recipient countries.

The upshot is that a rich menu of options exists for greater transatlantic coordination on China. Together, the United States and the EU account for nearly 50 percent of global GDP and more than 50 percent of global defense spending. The more Washington and Brussels can temper tensions in other areas of the relationship, the more they will be able to realize gains in their shared interest in shaping China's external behavior. To move in that direction, the United States will need to accept that Brussels has a different level of tolerance for friction with China and work to make progress where progress is possible, even if it is more likely to lead to steady incremental progress on specific issues than to some type of shared vision or grand strategy on China.

Pursue a Patient Approach with India

Developments in Sino-Indian relations have been marked by steady expansion of trade and investment flows and regular engagement at senior levels, all amid a constant low boil of tensions that occasionally rise to the surface. The most recent flare-up of tensions occurred at the Line of Actual Control in Ladakh in summer 2020, resulting in the first Chinese and Indian troop fatalities related to fighting in over forty years. Previous border incidents occurred in summer 2017, September 2014, April 2013, and repeatedly in previous years dating back to the Sino-Indian border war in 1962.

Areas of friction in the relationship extend well beyond boundary disputes, though. They also include economic and trade tensions. India has a $63 billion bilateral trade deficit with China, its largest with any trading partner in the world. India's frustrations with China's economic policies largely mirror American (and European) complaints. Tension is also mounting over technology issues as Chinese firms increasingly seek to push into India's market.

The two Asian powers also have tensions over water management of the Brahmaputra, which originates in the Chinese Himalayas and provides a vital source of water to the subcontinent. India's hosting of Tibetan exiles, most notably the Dalai Lama, remains a source of friction, as do China's expanding efforts to secure access to ports to India's east, south, and west. China's support for Pakistan is a key point of irritation. So, too, is China's obstruction of a greater role for India in international forums of which it is a member, notably the Nuclear Suppliers Group and the United Nations Security Council.

The endurance of these intractable challenges places a natural ceiling on how far Sino-Indian relations will develop. At the same time, leaders in Beijing and Delhi have both sought in recent years to search for fewer points of friction even as they have sought to avoid any appearance of giving ground. Delhi wishes to focus on its more pressing socioeconomic challenges at home, just as Beijing seeks to limit tensions with other powers to focus on challenges at home and with the United States.

India hopes a generally constructive relationship with China can lead to greater inbound investment from China and greater opportunity for Indian exports in China's market. India would like China to lessen its support for Pakistan and become less resistant to India playing a larger role in international bodies, but it is not counting on such an outcome. India's goal is to protect its privileged position in its near abroad, prevent any loss of its claimed territories, and promote a growing role for itself on the world stage. Foremost, though, India's foreign policy is designed to support its domestic objectives, chief among them raising the living standards of its people.

Any American effort to dramatically alter India's conception of its interests vis-à-vis China is likely to do more harm than good. First, as the India expert Tanvi Madan has described, "Delhi's view of China as a challenge has pre-dated those of many other major powers and has remained fairly consistent since the late 1950s. Second, there is a deep mistrust toward China among both policy makers and the Indian public. A spring 2019 Pew poll indicated that only 23% of Indians surveyed had a favorable view of China—lower than anywhere else other than Japan."[20] This distrust is baked into India's current approach toward China. Third, India jealously guards its strategic autonomy and avoids overreliance on outside powers for its own security. This is a long-standing feature of India's diplomatic tradition. It will not change anytime soon. Therefore India will be more likely to seek to preserve an equilibrium and avoid direct collision with China than to take an adversarial tack and depend on support from others to sustain it.

American engagement with India on China must be informed by these realities. As former U.S. ambassador to India Robert Blackwill and the India expert Ashley Tellis have argued, "If the United States' aim is to turn India into a close ally, formal or otherwise, it will come to grief. Instead, Washington and New Delhi should strive to forge a partnership oriented toward furthering common interests without expecting an alliance of any kind."[21]

The more confident New Delhi feels in the dependability of its relations with Washington, the less pull it will feel to diversify its international portfolio by improving relations with Beijing. Washington does not need New Delhi to seek to *block* China; it merely needs India to want to work with the United States and others to *balance* China. Substantive work along these lines could include enhanced U.S.-Indian collaboration in the development of cyber and space technologies, greater coordination on air and missile defense, and, at the higher end, willingness to allow each other's militaries to use facilities for rotational access.[22] Washington could also elevate efforts to support India's development of antisurface and antisubmarine capabilities, given its sensitivity to the growing presence of the PLA Navy in the Indian Ocean. Washington should also strongly support enhanced Indian participation in matters of global governance, including the United Nations Security Council.

Some in Washington are enthusiastic about the development of a quadrilateral grouping of the United States, India, Australia, and Japan as a means of balancing China. I am less enamored with this grouping, both because its symbolism has outpaced substantive output and will likely continue to do so for the foreseeable future, and also because it comes at costs to America's relations with other key actors (for example, Vietnam, Indonesia, Singapore, the Republic of Korea, and others), all of whom feel sidelined from conversations taking place at the "grown-up table." America's strategy in Asia should be to nurture a dense web of relationships involving all actors in the region, not a concert among the big democracies that leaves all others feeling marginalized, particularly since some of

America's most critical partners in the region are not consolidated democracies.

Returning to U.S.-India coordination on China, it will also be imperative for both countries jointly to encourage China to take on a greater role in addressing shared transnational challenges. Washington and New Delhi could urge Beijing to raise environmental, social, and labor standards for overseas development projects, particularly those funded through the AIIB and the New Development Bank; India is a founding member of both institutions. The United States and India could press China to elevate the prioritization of east–west infrastructure connectivity projects that link India with Southeast Asia and China. This could lessen the considerable sting to India of China's $60 billion investment in the China–Pakistan Economic Corridor, a massive project that establishes a north–south overland route from western China through disputed territory with India to Pakistan and ultimately the Indian Ocean via the port of Gwadar.

Whatever the specific modalities, the overall orientation of America's approach toward India should be guided by the principle that a strong, secure, confident India is in Washington's interest, even if New Delhi goes its own way on specific policy issues. America's priority for steadily strengthening coordination with India on China must override impulses to confront Delhi over lesser bilateral irritants. This will require America to exhibit patient farsightedness, trusting that closer U.S.-India relations will pay dividends over time in strengthening America's leverage for dealing with the more pressing strategic challenges posed by China's rise.

Build on Japan's Strengths

Tokyo yet again confronts a sense of vulnerability about its strategic position. Japan today faces an increasingly assertive and ascendant China, a North Korea that is steadily expanding its nuclear and missile inventories, and an increasingly inward-looking United States. In response, Tokyo has sought to anchor Japanese foreign policy in the U.S.-Japan relationship while also stabilizing relations with Beijing. Chinese and Japanese leaders have resumed direct engagement, and the governments of both countries have similarly been meeting to discuss the full spectrum of issues in the bilateral relationship.

Latent tensions over the Senkaku/Diaoyu Islands have remained elevated, with both China and Japan increasing their presence in the area; however, the frequency of Chinese incursions into contested waters and airspace has been occurring according to a predictable pattern, thereby lowering the risk of unintended incidents.[23] Technology competition has also emerged as a new source of friction, particularly after Tokyo's decision to ban the Chinese telecommunications company Huawei from its national system.

For Japan, South Korea and Taiwan serve as essential buffers against China. Tokyo is concerned that if either falls into China's orbit, Japan's strategic position would be significantly degraded. As an island nation with scarce natural resources, Japan depends on open sea lines of communication for imports of raw materials and exports to sustain its prosperity.

From Japan's standpoint, overreliance on the U.S. alliance exacerbates its abandonment/entrapment dilemma, wherein Japan risks either becoming isolated or being implicated in a war not of its choosing as a consequence of decisions made by the United States. Tokyo must constantly navigate between Scylla and Charybdis to avoid these twin challenges.

For China, Japan is an issue freighted with nationalistic emotion. The Chinese leadership keeps memories of Japan's World War II atrocities close to the surface through propaganda and commemorative anniversaries. Chinese officials also regularly lament the U.S.-Japan security alliance. Beijing recognizes that the alliance is the principal enabler of the United States' ability to project power throughout Northeast Asia. The alliance also strengthens Tokyo's leverage in its dealings with Beijing. Beijing resents both facts. It would like to see gaps between Tokyo and Washington emerge and widen over time, eventually leading Japan to prioritize relations with China over the United States.

China is Japan's largest trading partner. Japan surpassed all foreign investors in China in its cumulative investments between 1995 and 2017 with $101 billion. Thus, pursuing an adversarial approach is not a sensible posture for Tokyo, given the immense economic effects that would accompany any such strategy.[24]

At the same time, given Japan's complicated history with Beijing and its abandonment/entrapment dilemma with Washington, Tokyo must also seek to diversify its security and economic relationships. It has steadily pursued this course, deepening ties with India, the European Union, Australia, and others. Over time, Japan will aim to become a networked middle power that prudently manages risks while punching above its weight in certain areas, such as promoting free trade and pushing forward international standards, for example on quality infrastructure projects in third countries.[25]

Washington should welcome and encourage Tokyo to travel down this path, even if it results in Japan taking a less aggressive approach toward China than Washington would prefer. A secure, confident, and comfortable Japan will make a better partner for the United States in dealing with China over the long term than an anxious Japan that resents being pressured into positions that it would not otherwise take. Japan is America's most important ally in the most important region of the world for America's future. America's Asia strategy is built on the foundation of a strong U.S.-Japan alliance. For Washington, the path to East Asia goes through Tokyo. There is no alternative.

Washington and Tokyo should build on ongoing efforts to encourage a race-to-the-top dynamic with China on regional infrastructure development projects. Through its Quality Infrastructure

Investment Partnership, Japan has made major inroads in Southeast Asia by providing a transparent, environmentally friendly, and fiscally sustainable alternative to China's Belt and Road Initiative projects. According to a study by Fitch Solutions, Japan's economic footprint in Southeast Asia far exceeds China's. Japan has $367 billion in pending projects in the region, compared to $255 billion for China.[26] Partly as a result of the quality and quantity of its investments, Japan enjoys considerably more trust in Southeast Asia than any other country.[27] The United States should support Japan's Quality Infrastructure Investment Partnership, potentially through public-private funding contributions and joint projects with the United States International Development Finance Corporation.

Relatedly, Washington should also encourage Japan to concentrate its considerable capabilities on meeting infrastructure shortfalls in East Asia. Doing so would address an abundant demand and would also dilute Chinese attempts to geographically concentrate BRI projects along its immediate periphery. It is in both the United States' and Japan's interest to see China's overseas financing spread thinly across a wide geography, rather than concentrated to the point of becoming a source of overwhelming Chinese leverage with Southeast Asian recipient countries.

The United States should also support Japanese efforts to push China to reform economically to meet the requirements for entry into the Comprehensive and Progressive Agreement for Trans-Pacific Partnership (CPTPP). The incentive of entry into CPTPP holds a greater likelihood of encouraging China to undertake liberalizing market reforms than the disincentive of unilateral tariffs. One caveat, though: Washington should seek an understanding with Tokyo that Beijing will not be allowed to enter CPTPP ahead of the United States. If China jumps the line on entry into CPTPP, the United States would face a major competitive disadvantage.

Last, the United States should shift from wariness to support of Japan's pursuit of rapprochement with Russia. Under Putin, Russia has sought to shore up its identity as a great power by strengthening its position in Northeast Asia. Up to now, Russia's only entry point into Asia has been through deepening relations with China. Improvements in Russia-Japan relations would provide Moscow with more options for participating in regional affairs and also bolster Russia's severely diminished leverage with China and reduce Moscow's dependence on Beijing.

Play a Long Game with Russia

In recent decades, there has been an inverse relationship between Russia's relationship with the West and the closeness of its ties with China. As Russia's connections to the West have frayed, its willingness to make concessions to China in service of closer ties has grown. This dynamic has intensified under President Vladimir Putin and President Xi Jinping.

Putin resumed the presidency in May 2012, and Xi Jinping took control of China close to one year later. They both had to navigate unanticipated domestic turbulence as they entered office; Putin faced large-scale public protests against his return to power, and Xi had to contend with elite-level disunity at the top of the Communist Party.

Both leaders were also jarred by the Arab Spring. The spontaneous public protests that spread across the Arab world, and America's active support of them, triggered neuralgia in both men about domestic political and social stability. These events concentrated both leaders on their shared perception of the threat to their security posed by U.S. democracy promotion.

Xi made his first overseas trip to Moscow, and Putin soon reciprocated. In the years since, Xi and Putin have met more than thirty times, making Putin the foreign leader with whom Xi has met by far most often and, by all appearances, also the leader with whom Xi has established the greatest depth of shared understanding. Although the substance of their exchanges has evolved depending on

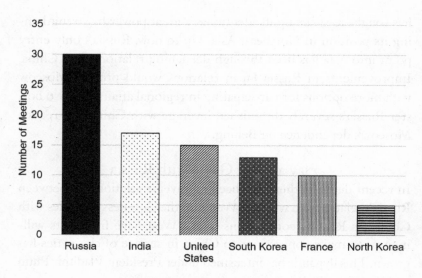

Xi Jinping's meetings by country, 2013–2020
Data from various media

events at home and abroad, the one continuous thread of their discussions has been domestic security and social stability. These are issues on which both leaders look at the world through the same eyes.

During a state dinner in honor of President Xi at the White House in September 2015, I was seated next to Xi's close advisor and de facto chief of staff, Li Zhanshu. Li is an enigmatic figure. At that time, he accompanied Xi on virtually all his major trips, often sat next to Xi in protocol order at official meetings, and almost never said anything within earshot of any American officials. Li did, however, serve as Xi's special envoy on several trips to Russia. This was abnormal in Chinese statecraft, given that Li was not a trained diplomat and did not have any known expertise on Russian affairs, beyond being a close advisor to Xi.

Over the course of the state dinner, I sought to draw Li out on his views, with little success. Li was perfectly amiable, though far more comfortable with pleasantries than substance. He deflected questions by talking about his nostalgia for the Chinese country-side and for the relative simplicity of his previous work as a local official in contrast with his responsibilities in Beijing. The one question that did arouse his response, though, was on the difference between senior-level Chinese engagements with Russia and with the United States. Li told me that the Chinese leadership consid-ered meetings with American officials as major events requiring significant preparation. There was no margin for error. U.S. lead-ers invariably were respectful, but also pointed, direct, and sharp. Traveling to Moscow, by contrast, was "comfortable" and "smooth." It felt like talking among friends who understood each other, he recounted.

Such a sense of friendship and mutual recognition of shared vul-nerabilities appears to have deepened after Russia's annexation of Crimea. According to former national intelligence officer for Russia Angela Stent, "The imposition of Western sanctions against Russia and the West's attempts to isolate it pushed Moscow more closely toward Beijing and increased Russia's dependence on China."[28] Bei-jing did not come to Moscow's aid in a time of need out of altruism, though. It drove a hard bargain in the process, exploiting Moscow's isolation to acquire defense systems that Russia had previously been unwilling to sell to China, and locking in terms for long-term oil contracts that Russia had rebuffed for years. The oil contract assured China of a steady supply of imports that do not need to travel by ship through strategic choke points (for example, the Strait of Malacca or the Gulf of Aden) that could be shut off by the U.S. Navy during a crisis. Russia now stands as China's largest sup-plier of petrochemicals in the world.

During the same period, U.S. relations with both Russia and China have simultaneously grown more antagonistic, despite Trump's personal efforts to forge closer personal relations with both Putin and Xi. During the Trump administration, the United States has launched a trade war with China at the same time as it has been ramping up sanctions on Russia. The U.S. Department of Defense has also trained a wary eye on Chinese and Russian military activities. Not unsurprisingly, Moscow and Beijing have responded by moving closer to each other across the board to shore up their ability to withstand pressure from the United States. For example, both have sought to lower their use of U.S. dollars for cross-border payments. In 2020, the share of dollar payments to clear China-Russia trade has fallen below 50 percent for the first time, and both sides have signaled determination to further reduce their use of dollars in the coming years.[29]

The United States has accelerated these trend lines by lumping China and Russia together as two sides of the same coin. Both the 2017 National Security Strategy and the 2018 National Defense Strategy presented China and Russia as being joint partners in seeking to erode American leadership and undermine democratic values around the world. This framing treated as a foregone conclusion that China and Russia have a common worldview and will work together to realize it, irrespective of any other factors.

The Trump administration's treatment of the Sino-Russian relationship as a new axis bent on challenging America's position globally is informed by a series of concerns. At the most basic level, America's disadvantageous position in the strategic triangle is a source of psychological stress, particularly for those in national security leadership positions within the U.S. government. For proponents of promoting democratic values around the world, deepening Sino-Russian relations represent a dangerous portent. "History (and research by the political scientists Carles Boix and Seva Gunitsky) show that when the world is led by one or more authoritarian powers, more countries become authoritarian."[30] Military planners are concerned that China and Russia are collaborating to strengthen their shared capacity to undermine America's ability to execute its operational plans in military contingencies around the world. Diplomats are frustrated by growing patterns of coordination between Moscow and Beijing, both on discrete foreign policy issues at the United Nations and elsewhere, and more broadly in their shared efforts to reshape the international order to better reflect their values and preferences. Intelligence agencies are concerned about Russian and Chinese collaboration in sharing sensitive information on American operations that are being conducted against them.[31] Grand strategists are similarly alarmed by the closeness of ties between Beijing and Moscow. Dating back to the British strategist Halford Mackinder's observation that whoever controlled the Eurasian landmass would control the world, a common feature of American strategy has been to seek to prevent any power or group of powers from dominating Eurasia.[32]

Even as there are strong impulses inside the U.S. government to drive a wedge between China and Russia, U.S. policy makers must resist the urge and instead play a long game with both countries. Any American attempt to create divisions between these two powers now would be more likely to push them together than pull them apart.

The objectives of American efforts over the near to mid-term should be to slow down the pace of convergence between Moscow and Beijing. This, in turn, will create space over time for natural sources of tension in the Sino-Russian relationship to resurface.

The China-Russia relationship is influenced by policy choices made in Washington, Brussels, and elsewhere. If Washington lumps both countries together and simultaneously pursues antagonistic policies toward both, it will likely cause both countries to move even closer to each other to counter the growing threat they perceive from Washington. It could lead, for example, to Russia deciding to put its global network of bases and military assets at China's disposal. Such a decision would dramatically alter Washington's assessment of the threat that China poses to America's global interests.[33]

If, on the other hand, Washington finds ways to keep both countries invested in the benefits (or deferred costs) of nonhostile relations, then it will raise the risk to both of taking further coordinated steps to challenge American interests. China has reasons of its own not to turn the dial up to ten in its relationship with Russia, unless China determines that there is no point in refraining from doing so, because the United States is determined to view China as its permanent enemy. As the China expert Stapleton Roy has observed, "China's leaders are acutely aware that overt hostility toward the United States would carry a major risk of compromising their strategic objective of keeping Taiwan within a one-China framework. . . . A decision by China to form a partnership with Russia that was clearly targeted against the United States would increase the likelihood that the United States would once again begin to view Taiwan as a strategic asset in dealing with an antagonistic China, thus undermining Beijing's unification goal."[34]

A similar set of calculations applies to Russia. If the United States removes all meaningful constraints on strategic competition with Russia and signals its indifference to striving for strategic stability, then it will lessen the risk for Moscow of seizing every opportunity to partner with Beijing in putting pressure on the United States. For this reason, the United States should reengage Moscow in arms control talks as a means of keeping Russia invested in addressing sources of insecurity, rather than push Russia away and pursue maximum advantage in the strategic domain instead.

The relationship between Russia and China is not developing along a predetermined path. By historical standards, Sino-Russian relations today are unnaturally close. Although leaders in both countries have a common set of grievances and paranoias, the two countries do not have a common worldview. Moscow believes it is a victim of the current international system, in which its economy and society stagnate while others around them race forward, and in response, Russia wants to break the current international order. Beijing, on the other hand, has gained wealth and power within the post–World War II international order. Beijing does not see benefit in trying to flip the table on the existing international order and absorbing the instability that would follow.

Given the investments that both Putin and Xi have made in the bilateral relationship, the two countries will likely remain close as long as one or both presidents remain in power. This suggests that it would not be realistic to expect that one country or the other will turn its back on Sino-Russian relations anytime soon. At the same time, it remains an open question how much closer the two countries might become, and whether Xi's and Putin's successors will follow the same approach to the triangular relationship. This is the space where the United States should focus its efforts, not by growing soft toward one or the other in hopes of eliciting reciprocal restraint, but rather by becoming more selective about where and when to apply pressure.

Conclusion

The displacement in the international system caused by China's rise is generating demand in the United States to develop a new grand strategy for responding. Against this backdrop, the prescriptions here may feel underambitious for the scale of the challenges being posed by China's rise. They should not. As long as other major and regional powers remain secure, confident, and comfortable in their relationships with the United States, their natural interests will militate toward balancing against China's rise; historical currents will end up pushing them and the United States in the same general direction. If, on the other hand, they grow uncomfortable with the onerousness of demands the United States places on them to confront China, or unsure of America's reliability as a steadfast partner, or unconvinced that they and the United States are bound by shared values, those same countries will hedge risk by moving closer to China.

The purpose of American strategy and policy with the European

Union and its major member countries, as well as with India and Japan, is to ensure that those nations remain confident in the United States and assured that they derive strategic value from remaining close to the United States. When these conditions are present, the focus of scrutiny will be on China's behavior. If, on the other hand, the United States abandons the values that bind it to its allies and chooses to confront China on its own, or pressures other countries to push back on China without duly considering their own interests vis-à-vis China, then the outcome would become far more uncertain.

Thus, for the United States, strengthening relationships with other major powers will require understanding and accepting how they each are perceiving China's rise, rather than seeking to impose its own threat calculus of China on others. Any attempt to convince other major powers that China is an implacable foe will do more to isolate the United States than to put pressure on China. No leaders in the European Union, India, and Japan subscribe to such a view.

At the same time, leaders in the European Union, India, and Japan generally remain invested in developing productive relations with the United States. They all share America's interest in seeing China refrain from coercion and accept greater burdens in addressing transnational challenges. This provides a strong base on which the United States can work with other major powers to craft a shared agenda for influencing how China identifies and pursues its interests.

Although this moment feels fraught with uncertainty, it is not the first time that the United States has had to reorient itself to address rising concerns about an erosion of American leadership on the world stage. In the 1964 editorial discussed earlier, the *New York Times* urged the United States to regain confidence in its ability to protect and promote its interests in a more competitive world. The *Times* wrote, "The materials with which to build a strong, trusted, influential foreign policy are all there. The power of the United

States is still unrivaled. What has to be learned is a way to use that power in a world which no longer accepts dictation or even leadership. Understanding, flexibility, adaptation, initiative—these are qualities the United States has not greatly needed in the past, yet they are the keys to peace, security, self-interest and prestige in today's world."[35] What was true then remains true today. As long as the United States musters the ability to fortify relationships with the European Union, India, and Japan while not gratuitously inflaming tensions with Russia, it will remain in a strong position to promote a favorable balance of power in the international system.

SEVEN

Moving Forward

The scale of the challenges that China poses to American interests and values demands that the United States develop a new strategy for China. In the process, however, the United States must guard against overcorrecting. Turning China into an enemy, such as by attempting to blunt its rise or destabilize its social system, would not be smart, sustainable, or strategic. Rather, the United States will need to recognize the competitive and interdependent nature of its relationship with China and concentrate on revitalizing its own sources of strength. Doing so will give the United States the best shot at being able to continue outpacing China economically and outshining its model of governance internationally.

Context

At the time of this writing, there is a deep and pervasive sense across many communities in America that things are not right. The COVID-19 pandemic has held up a mirror to the country and shown the holes in America's health-care system, social safety net, and economy. Manufacturing jobs are fading away, unemployment is pervasive, capital is being concentrated in isolated pockets of the economy, and access to opportunities is shrinking for an ever-widening swath of the population.[1] President Donald Trump is not the source of these trends. But he has keenly understood the insecurity that many Americans feel, and his politics speak to that insecurity.

President Trump has made China a part of his political brand. A new policy orientation has flowed from Trump's determination to project strength in dealing with China. The Trump administration has adopted great power competition as the organizing principle of American foreign policy, much as containment served as a north star for American policy during the Cold War and countering violent extremism animated America's efforts in the decade after the September 11 terrorist attacks. Many proponents of great power competition hope that the concept will have a disciplining effect, helping American policy makers resist impulses to get drawn into peripheral problems and instead remain focused on the big challenge: China, and to a lesser extent, Russia.[2]

This has been a cathartic policy transformation for many American policy practitioners and analysts who have been concerned by the rapidity of China's rise and the seeming lack of urgency in America's response. It has also been a welcome shift for many Americans who have been angered by the seeming impunity with which China has committed human rights violations against its own citizens. Trump's unconventional approach has broken the mold of forty years of America's policy toward China, opening space for debate and new thinking on assumptions and objectives that should guide American strategy. Such openness to challenging past practices is a healthy feature of America's diplomatic tradition, one that gives the United States a comparative advantage over China, which, owing to the character of its one-party system and its concentrated decision-making around Xi Jinping, cannot easily or quickly obtain unvarnished feedback, acknowledge previous errors in judgment by the top leadership, and nimbly adjust policy to adapt to changing circumstances.

Costs and Consequences of Turning China into a Hostile Adversary

While fresh thinking on how best to contend with China is necessary and overdue, this process must also be leavened by an awareness of the risks of allowing the pendulum to swing too far toward alarmism. If such a trend is left unchecked, the United States risks overcorrecting in a manner that could lead to more harm than benefit.

Some analysts have argued that such concerns are moot, because China already views the United States through an ideological prism and sees America as its foremost challenger. Therefore, according to the argument, it is only right and fair for the United States to reciprocate. These arguments contain a grain of truth. Chinese leaders do view the United States as Beijing's foremost competitor. Even so, foreign policy is not guided by schoolyard codes of disliking others because they dislike you. It is guided by realpolitik and pursuit of national interest. And if the United States chooses to define China as its existential enemy, then it will change the world, and America's place in it, with significant negative repercussions for American national interests.

First, any decision to approach China as a Cold War–like adversary will generate pressure to mobilize to counter the threat. If past is prologue, we will see heightened efforts to scrutinize activities of ethnic Chinese who are residing legally in the United States, as well as Americans deemed to be sympathetic to Chinese aims. Historically, this has been the pattern when the United States has faced challenges in the past from Germany, Japan, and the Soviet Union. Indeed, FBI director Christopher Wray has already warned in congressional testimony in 2018 that the United States must mobilize to counter the "whole of society" threat being posed by China.[3]

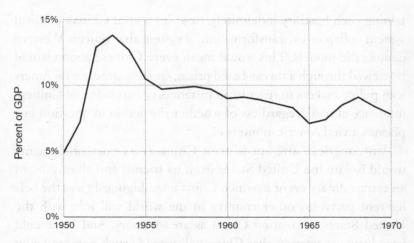

U.S. historical defense spending as a percentage of GDP, 1950–1970
Data from U.S. Office of Management and Budget

We will also see a push to elevate defense spending to regain an edge over Chinese forces. As a point of comparison, in the years after the onset of the Cold War, U.S. military spending skyrocketed.

If such a cycle were to repeat itself today, it would starve the U.S. government of funds to address pressing domestic needs, including funding for basic science research, improving access to health care, and overdue infrastructure upgrades. And unlike at the outset of the Cold War, American society today has no figure of Dwight Eisenhower's stature and military background capable of sounding the alarm and rallying political support for reining in defense spending, as Eisenhower famously did in 1961.[4] Simply put, the United States cannot afford to dramatically ramp up defense spending and at the same time make the types of overdue domestic investments necessary to restore the country as a democratic beacon for the rest of the world. It will have to choose.

If the United States crosses the Rubicon of defining China as its existential enemy, it will almost certainly need to persist in maintaining such hostility indefinitely, or at least until China's political system collapses or transforms into a system that reflects Western democratic models. This would mean every Chinese action would be viewed through a threat-based prism, creating pressure on American policy makers to react to all instances of expansion of Chinese influence abroad, regardless of whether the action in question implicates a vital American interest.

Any American attempt to treat China as its existential enemy would isolate the United States from its friends and allies. Absent an extraordinary event in which China unambiguously was the belligerent party, no other country in the world will join with the United States in treating China as an adversary. And we should have little expectation that China will provide such a crystallizing moment. Even American allegations of official Chinese complicity in the spread of COVID-19 will likely not play such a galvanizing role, given the persistent scientific ambiguity about the origin of the virus.

Senior Chinese officials have told me and others privately for some time that if the United States launches a new Cold War, it should not expect China to show up for it. Beijing is determined to deprive Washington of the ability to divide the world into competing blocs vying for global influence.

If the United States travels down such a path on its own, it will struggle to resist treating its relationships with allies and friends as derivative of its competition with China. Already such impulses are becoming visible, as relations with erstwhile allies have come under strain based partly on those nations' unwillingness to adopt America's threat perception of China. A good example is America's threat to cut off intelligence sharing with the United Kingdom if it does not ban Huawei 5G telecommunications technology from its national grid.[5]

An American judgment of China as its enemy would also tear at the fabric of the global economy. Given the globally integrated nature of supply chains, any American attempt to reroute production outside of China would generate inefficiencies and additional costs. Such a process has already begun on a smaller scale with labor-intensive production and as part of America's efforts to secure its defense industrial supply chain from dependence on any Chinese inputs.[6] Extending such efforts to the entire American economy, or even a large segment of it, would introduce significant economic volatility. Attempting to compel other countries to follow America's lead would inject even more stress into the global economy, to say nothing of America's economic and diplomatic relationships with other major trading partners.

It also is important to recall that the U.S.-China relationship is dynamic, not one-sided. Beijing has a say in the conduct of the relationship. When, for example, the Trump administration launched trade tariffs against China, Beijing retaliated immediately with geographically targeted tariffs designed to inflict maximal pain on constituencies that were key to Trump's political standing. Similarly, if Washington settles on an approach of unmitigated rivalry in furtherance of great power competition, it will likely compel Beijing to remove restraints on its own actions toward the United States.

China has ample ways to inflict retaliatory harm on the United States short of direct military hostilities. For example, Beijing could step up pressure on pro-U.S. governments in Asia and farther afield to evict U.S. troops or create distance with Washington, dial up coercion on Taiwan to accept unification, proactively support North Korean and Iranian nuclearization plans, become more active in asserting control over Hong Kong, undermine the global nonproliferation regime, seek to mobilize ethnic Chinese populations overseas to sow discord, conduct disruptive cyber operations against U.S. infrastructure or institutions of trust, provide material support to nongovernmental groups with hostile intentions toward the United States, nationalize U.S. factories inside China, and harass and detain American citizens in China. The depth of entanglement between the two powers generates significant mutual vulnerabilities that could be exploited short of kinetic conflict if the relationship deteriorates into outright enmity.

Striking a Balance between Dismissiveness and Alarmism

Fortunately, the United States does not need to travel down this path. The United States does not need to harm China to help itself. A wiser, steadier path for coping with China while strengthening the United States is within grasp.

Getting to a better path will not be easy, though. The United States does not have the option of turning back the clock to 2016 and treating the intervening years as an aberration. The United States, China, and the world have already changed too much. The scale of China's repression at home, assertiveness abroad, and willingness to employ economic coercion to achieve political objectives has rendered the previous American approach insufficient to the challenge China now presents.

Taking a softer approach to China and expecting China to reciprocate also is unlikely to yield desired results. Any approach that resembles appeasement, in addition to being politically untenable, would more likely elicit Chinese boundary testing than Chinese restraint. In such a scenario, Beijing would push until it hit steel, escalate rhetorical and economic threats, evaluate America's response, and then adjust course if needed.[7] Beijing would almost certainly feel compelled to determine the outer limits of how far it could push the U.S. presence out of the western Pacific, including challenging America's alliance relationships in the region. This would be an instability-inducing process.

A wiser, steadier path for dealing with China's rise would require U.S. leaders to accept that the United States will not be able to impose its will on China, short of risking catastrophic conflict, and at the same time, it will not have the resources or focus necessary to achieve its national ambitions if it is engaged in an outright hostile relationship with China. The same holds true for China with the United States. This entanglement imposes boundaries on the relationship, creating conditions of competitive interdependence, where competition is the defining feature and interdependence is inescapable. Each will seek to nudge the other in a preferred direction, and a continuous push-and-pull dynamic will prevail across the Pacific and around the globe. Neither will ever be fully satisfied with the other, but both will be forced to find ways to coexist, largely out of an acknowledgment that there are no tenable alternatives.

A Case for American Self-Confidence

The key question, therefore, is not which side will prevail over the other, but rather whether and how the United States will be able to strengthen its ability to outpace China economically and outshine China in terms of its social and political model. The manner in which the United States responds to China's rise will be determined in large part by America's confidence in itself and in its place in the world. Just as George Kennan identified patience as the indispensable feature of America's strategy for coping with the Soviet Union during the Cold War, in this time of testing, self-confidence will be a key factor—perhaps *the* key factor—in America's ability to manage China's rise.

Confidence is the wellspring of patience and steadiness. It is what helps buffer the United States from swinging between the poles of dismissiveness and alarmism on China. It is what allows the United States to temper and manage disputes rather than clumsily attempt to dictate outcomes. It is what helps policy makers distinguish between Chinese actions that challenge vital American interests and must be contested and those that do not. Confidence also helps leaders appreciate that relations between major powers are rarely punctuated by splashy public breakthroughs but rather are guided by thousands of day-to-day decisions in service of broader strategic aims.

Confidence is *the* essential ingredient for guarding against American overreaction to China's rise, with all its attendant risks in the form of alienation, miscalculation, and enmity. The more confident the United States is in its ability to compete, the more capable it will be of charting a durable course for dealing with China.

The United States has ample reasons to maintain confidence in its ability to compete with China: an economy that is $7 trillion larger than China's; energy and food security; comparatively healthy demographics; the world's finest higher-education system; peaceful borders; the world's reserve currency; an economy that allocates capital efficiently and serves as a sponge for the brightest thinkers and best ideas in the world; a transparent and predictable legal system; and a historically unmatched set of alliances that cover 75 percent of global GDP and defense spending.

China, by contrast, represents the hardest governance challenge on the planet. It faces strong demographic headwinds, a cooling economy, inefficient capital markets, a rent-seeking regulatory environment that places a drag on innovation, a sclerotic political system that is becoming more ideological, and a looming environmental bill for the massive degradation that Chinese authorities allowed during their sprint of breakneck economic development. China's leaders must also contend with bubbling ethnic tensions across the country, the internal friction caused by the seeming removal of checks on Xi Jinping's authority, and the dearth of historical precedents for countries run by strongmen turning out well. China must also manage deepening fissures with Taiwan and Hong Kong, a range of territorial disputes, and an array of anxious middle powers surrounding China that are unwilling to subordinate their interests in deference to Chinese power.

China has also benefited over the past two decades from a unique set of circumstances that have allowed it to close the gap in national power with the United States faster than most analysts in the United States or China would have believed possible at the turn of the century. While some closing of the gap has resulted from Chinese choices, many Chinese experts I have spoken with since leaving government have attributed a greater share of the progress China has achieved to a series of strategic blunders by the United States. The U.S. invasion of Iraq in 2003 damaged America's international image and diverted focus away from Asia and to the Middle East. America's inability to achieve its strategic objectives in Afghanistan revealed the limits of American military power. The global financial crisis in 2008 sowed doubts around the world about the wisdom of America's political and economic model. American encouragement of democratic uprisings across the Middle East (the Arab Spring) drove refugee flows into Europe and contributed to a rise in nationalist populism. The surprise election of Donald Trump in 2016 intensified domestic divisions within the United States and led to a diminishment of American exercise of leadership on the world stage. Cumulatively, these setbacks sapped America's strength and confidence and created space for China's rise.

None of these facts diminish China's record over recent decades of amassing wealth, power, and prestige, nor do they lessen the challenges China will pose going forward. But the United States does not get to decide China's fate. The United States only has control over its own. And for its own, China is not the principal challenge facing the United States. If the United States wants to outpace and outshine China, its best path to doing so is by focusing on its own domestic renewal.

The reality and scale of the China challenge can be incrementally useful in alerting the U.S. body politic about the importance of undertaking domestic renewal, but the project will ultimately need to be justified on its own terms, not as a means for addressing an overinflated threat. Any effort to use the external threat of China as a basis for overcoming divisions at home is unlikely to succeed and likely to cause harm.

Unlike with the Soviet Union during the Cold War, there is not a broadly held view in the United States today that China poses an existential threat. Even as we see rising dissatisfaction with Chinese behavior, there is not public support for treating China as an adversary, and there is even less enthusiasm for bearing material burdens in service of confrontation with China.[8] This means that inflating the China threat is likely to have a far less galvanizing effect toward greater political unity than most of its proponents hope for. Furthermore, invoking China as the big external threat to trigger domestic unity will come at a cost, both in widening divisions between the United States and its allies and partners on China, and in inflaming tensions with China. American leaders cannot expect to bash China at home and not see repercussions abroad.

Breaking the Fever of American Political Polarization

Rather than fixating on China, America's leaders will need to focus on the root of the problem inside the United States. The current era of hyperpartisanship is the source of much of the dysfunction in America's political system today. Politicians have learned that playing on divisions earns them more attention, media coverage, fundraising, and partisan passion than compromising with counterparts across the aisle to achieve incremental progress on problems.

The costs and consequences of America's intensifying political polarization can be felt at home and abroad. At home, growing polarization has resulted in an inability of the federal government to address even the most glaring problems, like decaying infrastructure, an immigration system that needs reform, insufficient funding for basic research, and unequal access to opportunity. No less troublingly abroad, American diplomacy is being infected by intensifying partisanship. As the former American diplomat Bill Burns has observed, such polarization has led to a dynamic whereby "policies lurch between parties, commitments expire at the end of each administration, institutions are politicized, and disagreements are tribal. The inability to compromise at home is becoming the modus operandi overseas. In the past, a sense of common domestic purpose gave ballast to U.S. diplomacy, now its absence enfeebles it."[9]

Neither political party and no single politician own exclusive blame for these shortcomings. The national calluses hobbling the United States have built up over decades. Although state and local governments have proved resilient and capable of filling gaps, they alone cannot compensate for the national-level political system's failures.[10]

The American people are ahead of their politicians on many of these issues. A close review of polling is striking for the level of consensus that already exists in identifying the way forward on many of the social, economic, and foreign problems facing the United States. For example, Gallup polling has found that by a margin of 74 percent to 21 percent, the American people believe trade offers an opportunity to spur economic growth through exports. Eighty-three percent of Americans believe that undocumented adults brought to the United States as children, known as "dreamers," should be protected from deportation. Roughly 80 percent of citizens believe that humans are driving climate change. And as climate change denialism runs out of steam and the debate shifts from whether to what needs to be done, China will be at the center of discussion. Perhaps in part for this reason, nearly 70 percent of Americans believe Washington should pursue "friendly cooperation and engagement with China."[11] Taken together, these results highlight that pragmatism still exists among the American people, if not necessarily among the leaders they have elected.

For decades, the mark of the American system has been its ability to solve hard challenges, often not as efficiently as one would hope and not on linear paths according to preset plans, but eventually quite effectively. America's international prestige has been burnished by its domestic performance in improving the lives of its citizens and unlocking world-changing innovations.

America's economic model comes up for questioning every time the United States confronts a competitor with a state-led economic model. Despite its chaotic nature, or perhaps because of it, the American model has shown time and again its capacity for creativity and dynamism. The same country that sent a man to the moon and invented the internet still exists. It is underperforming relative to its potential right now, but even so, it still retains a commanding advantage over all other countries in its power, prosperity, and capacity to inspire.

When the political pendulum swings back to a more normal resting place and practical problem-solving regains relevance, a healthy to-do list of actions will await America's leaders. These include organizing efforts at home and abroad to stamp out COVID-19 and then using the opportunity created by the crisis to make long-term investments in strengthening American society—in schools, basic and applied research, public health, and clean energy. If American leaders do these things, or even shows signs of moving in these directions, they will revive global confidence in the power of America's example.

In the interim, U.S. leaders, policy makers, and the public will need to cling to the confidence that comes with knowing that even in spite of its flaws, the United States remains the indisputably dominant power in the U.S.-China relationship, and by a large margin. America retains abundant capacity to protect its vital interests while living with an increasingly powerful China. The United States need not—and should not—turn China into a hostile adversary. American interests will be better served by a durable, forthright, and productive relationship with China, where both sides preserve capacity to collaborate on shared challenges that neither can solve on its own even as they compete vigorously within a mutual acknowledgment of their interdependence.

John Lewis Gaddis, the dean of Cold War historians, reflected on America's sources of strength during its competition with the Soviet Union. In an interview for a May 2020 article in the *New*

Yorker, Gaddis observed, "America's advantage over the Soviet Union hinged less on aggression than competent government. The country can be no stronger in the world than it is at home. This was the basis for projecting power on the world scene. We [the United States] have lost that at home right now."[12]

The principal challenge for the United States is to "measure up to its own best traditions," in the words of George Kennan.[13] America's future prosperity and security will be determined by its own decisions and actions, not by Beijing's behavior. Similarly, the future character of the international system will be influenced by whether the United States demonstrates capacity for national cohesion in solving societal challenges. The more success the United States demonstrates at home, the stronger its influence will be felt across the rest of the international system.

Notes

Introduction

1. Ken Silverstein, "The Man from ONA," *The Nation*, October 7, 1999, https://www.thenation.com/article/archive/man-ona.
2. See Samuel Huntington, "The U.S.—Decline or Renewal?" *Foreign Affairs*, December 1, 1988.
3. Richard Fontaine, "Great-Power Competition Is Washington's Top Priority—but Not the Public's: China and Russia Don't Keep Most Americans Awake at Night," *Foreign Affairs*, September 9, 2019.

ONE
America's Enduring Strengths

1. Jeremy Diamond, "Trump: 'We Can't Continue to Allow China to Rape Our Country,'" CNN, May 2, 2016, https://www.cnn.com/2016/05/01/politics /donald-trump-china-rape/index.html.
2. Nate Cohn, "Trump's Electoral College Edge Could Grow in 2020, Rewarding Polarizing Campaign," *New York Times*, July 19, 2019, https://www .nytimes.com/2019/07/19/upshot/trump-electoral-college-edge-.html.
3. See, e.g., "Avoiding War: Containment, Competition, and Cooperation in US-China Relations," Brookings Interview, https://www.brookings.edu/wp -content/uploads/2017/11/fp_20171121_china_interview.pdf.

4. See Rush Doshi, "Hu's to Blame for China's Foreign Assertiveness?" (Washington, D.C.: Brookings Institution, January 2019), https://www.brookings.edu/articles/hus-to-blame-for-chinas-foreign-assertiveness.

5. See Robert Kagan, *The Jungle Grows Back: America and Our Imperiled World* (New York: Vintage Books, 2019); as well as Tarun Chhabra, "The China Challenge, Democracy, and US Grand Strategy" (Washington, D.C.: Brookings Institution, February 2019), https://www.brookings.edu/research/the-china-challenge-democracy-and-u-s-grand-strategy.

6. See James Mann, *The China Fantasy* (New York: Viking, 2007).

7. Edward Alden, *Failure to Adjust: How Americans Got Left Behind in the Global Economy* (Lanham, Md.: Rowman & Littlefield, 2017), 38.

8. See Elizabeth Thom, "New Survey Reveals an Anxious and Nostalgic America Going into the 2016 Election" (Washington, D.C.: Brookings Institution, November 2015), https://www.brookings.edu/blog/fixgov/2015/11/18/new-survey-reveals-an-anxious-and-nostalgic-america-going-into-the-2016-election; Bruce Stokes, "Global Publics More Upbeat about the Economy: But Many Are Pessimistic about Children's Future" (Washington, D.C.: Pew Research Center, June 2017), http://assets.pewresearch.org/wp-content/uploads/sites/2/2017/06/29161335/Pew-Research-Center-Economy-Report-FINAL-June-5-2017-UPDATED.pdf.

9. Tom Hertz, "Understanding Mobility in America" (Washington, D.C: Center for American Progress, April 2006), https://www.americanprogress.org/wp-content/uploads/kf/hertz_mobility_analysis.pdf.

10. Richard Hernandez, "The Fall of Employment in the Manufacturing Sector," U.S. Department of Labor, Bureau of Labor Statistics, August 2018, https://www.bls.gov/opub/mlr/2018/beyond-bls/the-fall-of-employment-in-the-manufacturing-sector.htm.

11. Federica Cocco, "Most US Manufacturing Jobs Lost to Technology, Not Trade," *Financial Times*, December 2, 2016, https://www.ft.com/content/dec677c0-b7e6-11e6-ba85-95d1533d9a62.

12. Ljubica Nedelkoska and Glenda Quintini, "Automation, Skills Use and Training," OECD Social, Employment and Migration Working Papers, no. 202 (Paris: OECD Publishing, 2018), https://doi.org/10.1787/2e2f4eea-en.

13. Kai-Fu Lee, *AI Superpowers: China, Silicon Valley, and the New World Order* (New York: Houghton Mifflin Harcourt, 2018), 164.

14. William H. Frey, "The US Will Become 'Minority White' in 2045, Census Projects" (Washington, D.C.: Brookings Institution, March 2018), https://www.brookings.edu/blog/the-avenue/2018/03/14/the-us-will-become-minority-white-in-2045-census-projects.

15. Mike Pence, "Remarks by Vice President Pence on the Administration's Policy toward China," Washington, D.C., October 4, 2018, https://www.whitehouse.gov/briefings-statements/remarks-vice-president-pence-administrations-policy-toward-china.

16. China's economy has decelerated from 10.6 percent GDP growth to 6.1 percent from 2010 to 2019, according to data from the International Monetary Fund: https://www.imf.org/external/datamapper/NGDP_RPCH@WEO/CHN.

17. China's GDP grew from $12.143 trillion (2017) to 13.608 trillion (2018), an increase of $1.465 trillion. Australia's economy (2018): $1.432 trillion. See World Bank data at https://data.worldbank.org/indicator/NY.GDP.MKTP.CD?locations=CN-AU.

18. China's contributions to global economic growth have grown from 9.2 percent of overall global growth in 2010 to 16.3 percent in 2019, according to data from the International Monetary Fund: https://www.imf.org/external/datamapper/NGDPD@WEO/WEOWORLD/CHN.

19. Charles Edel and Siddharth Mohandas, "Not Quite China's Century? An Early Appraisal," *National Interest*, November 20, 2018, https://nationalinterest.org/feature/not-quite-chinas-century-early-appraisal-36562.

20. Stephen Roach, "Flailing at China," Project Syndicate, August 27, 2019, https://www.project-syndicate.org/commentary/trump-incoherent-china-policies-by-stephen-s-roach-2019-08.

21. Derek Scissors, "China's Economic 'Miracle' in Context" (Washington, D.C.: American Enterprise Institute, August 2019), https://www.aei.org/research-products/report/chinas-economic-miracle-in-context.

22. Michael Beckley, *Unrivaled: Why America Will Remain the World's Sole Superpower* (Ithaca, N.Y.: Cornell University Press, 2018), 131–132.

23. "China Debt Ratio Is Growing as Its Economy Loses Steam," Bloomberg, July 16, 2019, https://www.bloomberg.com/news/articles/2019-07-16/china-s-debt-growth-keeps-marching-on-as-economy-loses-pace.

24. Ryan Avent, "China Is Not the Economic Superpower People Think," *Washington Post*, December 23, 2018, https://www.washingtonpost.com/business/economy/china-is-not-the-economic-superpower-people-think-thats-why-its-important-to-wait-it-out/2018/12/21/cf9999bc-03b1-11e9-b6a9-0aa5c2fcc9e4_story.html.

25. Jonathan Pollack and Jeff Bader, "Looking Before We Leap: Weighing the Risks of US-China Disengagement" (Washington, D.C.: Brookings Institution, July 2019), https://www.brookings.edu/research/looking-before-we-leap-weighing-the-risks-of-us-china-disengagement.

26. See, e.g., speech by Xi Jinping, "Deepening Exchanges and Mutual Learning among Civilizations for an Asian Community with a Shared Future," Beijing, China, May 15, 2019, https://www.fmprc.gov.cn/mfa_eng/wjdt_665385/zyjh_665391/t1663857.shtml.

27. Benjamin Shobert, *Blaming China: It Might Feel Good but It Won't Fix America's Economy* (Lincoln, Neb.: Potomac Books, 2019), 48.

28. Charles Edel, "Limiting Chinese Aggression: A Strategy of Counter-pressure," *American Interest*, February 9, 2018 (italics mine), https://www.the-american

-interest.com/2018/02/09/limiting-chinese-aggression-strategy-counter
-pressure.
29. Beckley, *Unrivaled*, 105.
30. Beckley, *Unrivaled*, 1.
31. Yan Xuetong, "How China Can Defeat America," *New York Times*, November 20, 2011, https://www.nytimes.com/2011/11/21/opinion/how-china
-can-defeat-america.html.
32. James Kitfield, "China's Bid for Asian Domination," Yahoo News, July 18, 2019, https://ph.news.yahoo.com/chinas-bid-for-asian-domination-the-view
-from-us-indo-pacific-command-222849711.html.
33. Beckley, *Unrivaled*, 1.
34. See Soumitra Dutta et al., *Global Innovation Index 2019* (Geneva, Switzerland: WIPO, 2019), https://www.wipo.int/publications/en/details.jsp?id=4434.
35. See data from Bank for International Settlements, "Triennial Central Bank Survey of Foreign Exchange and Over-the-Counter (OTC) Derivatives Markets in 2019," BIS, December 8, 2019, https://www.bis.org/statistics
/rpfx19.htm.
36. U.S. Energy Information Administration, "The U.S. Leads Global Petroleum and Natural Gas Production with Record Growth in 2018," USEIA, August 20, 2019, https://www.eia.gov/todayinenergy/detail.php?id=40973.
37. Michael J. Green, *By More than Providence: Grand Strategy and American Power in the Asia Pacific since 1783* (New York: Columbia University Press, 2017), 2.

TWO
China's Strategic Ambitions

1. Alastair Iain Johnston, "Shaky Foundations: The Intellectual Architecture of Trump's China Policy," *Survival* 61, no. 2 (March 2019): 1XY89–202.
2. See, e.g., Donald J. Trump, *National Security Strategy* (NSS) (Washington, D.C.: White House, 2017), https://www.whitehouse.gov/wp-content/uploads
/2017/12/NSS-Final-12-18-2017-0905.pdf; Mike Pence, "Remarks by Vice President Pence on the Administration's Policy toward China," Washington, D.C., October 4, 2018, https://www.whitehouse.gov/briefings-statements
/remarks-vice-president-pence-administrations-policy-toward-china.
3. Aaron Friedberg, *A Contest for Supremacy: China, America, and the Struggle for Mastery in Asia* (New York: W. W. Norton, 2012), 5–7.
4. Thomas Christensen, *The China Challenge* (New York: W. W. Norton, 2015), 53–54.
5. Bonnie S. Glaser and Matthew P. Funaiole, "The 19th Party Congress: A More Assertive Chinese Foreign Policy," *Lowy Interpreter*, October 26, 2017. See also Rush Doshi, "China's Role in Reshaping the International Financial

Architecture," in *Strategic Asia 2019: China's Expanding Strategic Ambitions* (Washington, D.C.: National Bureau of Asian Research, January 2019).

6. See, e.g., Elizabeth Economy, *The Third Revolution* (Oxford: Oxford University Press, 2018).

7. Ashley J. Tellis, Alison Szalwinski, and Michael Wills, *Understanding Strategic Cultures in the Asia-Pacific* (Seattle: National Bureau of Asian Research, 2016), 36.

8. Deng's original "twenty-four-character strategy" is further explored in Bradley A. Thayer and John M. Friend, "The China Threat and What the U.S. Should Do about It," *Strategy Bridge*, August 1, 2017, https://thestrategy bridge.org/the-bridge/2017/8/1/the-china-threat-what-the-us-should-do -about-it.

9. Wang Hui, "The Economy of Rising China and Its Contradictions," trans. David Ownby, *Reading the China Dream*, 2010, https://www.readingthechina dream.com/wang-hui-the-economy-of-rising-china.html.

10. Ci Jiwei, *Democracy in China: The Coming Crisis* (Cambridge, Mass.: Harvard University Press, 2019), 2.

11. Dai Bingguo, "Adhere to the Path of Peaceful Development," Xinhua News Agency, December 6, 2010.

12. Wang Jisi, "China's Search for a Grand Strategy," *Foreign Affairs*, March–April 2011, https://www.foreignaffairs.com/articles/china/2011-02-20/chinas -search-grand-strategy.

13. Xi Jinping, *Xi Jinping: The Governance of China* (Beijing, China: Foreign Language Press, 2014), 479.

14. Fu Ying, "China's Vision for the World: A Community of Shared Future, *The Diplomat*, June 22, 2017, https://thediplomat.com/2017/06/chinas-vision-for -the-world-a-community-of-shared-future.

15. Yang Jiechi, "Study and Implement General Secretary Xi Jinping's Thought on Diplomacy in a Deep-Going Way and Keep Writing New Chapters of Major-Country Diplomacy with Distinctive Chinese Features," *Xinhua*, July 17, 2017, http://www.xinhuanet.com/english/2017-07/19/c_136456009 .htm.

16. Xi Jinping, "Secure a Decisive Victory in Building a Moderately Prosperous Society in All Respects and Strive for the Great Success of Socialism with Chinese Characteristics for a New Era," Beijing, China, October 18, 2017, http://www.xinhuanet.com/english/download/Xi_Jinping's_report_at _19th_CPC_National_Congress.pdf.

17. See, e.g., Matthew J. Belvedere, "Opposites Attract: Even Steve Bannon and Tom Friedman Agree Trump Is Right to Attack on China Trade," CNBC, May 15, 2019, https://www.cnbc.com/2019/05/15/steve-bannon-and-thomas -friedman-agree-on-china-and-twitter-goes-nuts.html.

18. Jessica Chen Weiss, "A World Safe for Autocracy?" *Foreign Affairs* 98, no. 4

(July–August 2019), https://www.foreignaffairs.com/articles/china/2019-06
-11/world-safe-autocracy.

19. For example, see "Sharp Power: Rising Authoritarian Influence," National
Endowment for Democracy, December 5, 2017, https://www.ned.org/sharp
-power-rising-authoritarian-influence-forum-report.

20. Robert Kagan, *The Jungle Grows Back: America and Our Imperiled World* (New
York: Vintage Books, 2019), 151.

21. Kagan, *The Jungle Grows Back*, 147.

22. Xi Jinping, "Secure a Decisive Victory."

23. Zhou Jinghao, "China's Core Interests and Dilemma in Foreign Policy Practice," *Pacific Focus* 34, no. 1 (April 2019): 31–54.

24. Wang, "China's Search."

25. Fu Ying, *Seeing the World* (Beijing, China: CITIC Press Corporation, 2019),
26–27 (italics mine).

26. Evan Feigenbaum, "Reluctant Stakeholder: Why China's Highly Strategic
Brand of Revisionism Is More Challenging Than Washington Thinks," Car-
negie Endowment for International Peace, April 27, 2018, https://carnegie
endowment.org/2018/04/27/reluctant-stakeholder-why-china-s-highly
-strategic-brand-of-revisionism-is-more-challenging-than-washington
-thinks-pub-76213.

27. A leading Chinese international relations scholar, not-for-attribution conversation, Singapore, June 20, 2019.

28. Policy options available to Beijing for pulling Taiwan closer to the mainland
short of use of force include using economic threats and inducements;
squeezing Taiwan's diplomatic space, e.g., by pulling diplomatic allies away
from Taiwan; conducting enhanced military training operations in the vicin-
ity of Taiwan; placing pressure on Taiwanese firms that conduct business
operations on the mainland; and pressuring multinational firms that operate
in both Taiwan and the mainland to adopt the mainland's preferred nomen-
clature for referring to Taiwan.

29. "Impeachment Shows Hypocrisy of Partisan Politics," *Global Times*, December 19, 2019, https://www.globaltimes.cn/content/1174159.shtml. See also
Lu Hui, "Commentary: Chinese Democracy Puts Western Illusion in Dust,"
Xinhua, March 3, 2019, http://www.xinhuanet.com/english/2019-03/03/c
_137865763.htm.

30. See, e.g., Rush Doshi, "China's Global Information Influence Operations"
(Washington, D.C.: Brookings Institution, forthcoming).

31. Jeff Li, "China's History of Extraordinary Rendition," BBC News, June 16,
2019, https://www.bbc.com/news/world-asia-china-48634136.

32. See, e.g., Ketian Vivian Zhang, "Chinese Non-military Coercion—Tactics and
Rationale," Brookings Institution, January 22, 2019, https://www.brookings
.edu/articles/chinese-non-military-coercion-tactics-and-rationale.

33. Bruce Jones, "China and the Return of Great Power Strategic Competition"

(Washington, D.C.: Brookings Institution, February 2020), https://www
.brookings.edu/wp-content/uploads/2020/02/FP_202002_china_power
_competition_jones.pdf.

34. Shivshankar Menon, "How China Bucked Western Expectations and What
It Means for World Order" (Washington, D.C.: Brookings Institution,
March 10, 2016), https://www.brookings.edu/blog/order-from-chaos/2016
/03/10/how-china-bucked-western-expectations-and-what-it-means-for
-world-order.

35. Jonathan Stromseth, "The Testing Ground: China's Rising Influence in
Southeast Asia and Regional Responses" (Washington, D.C.: Brookings Institution, November 2019), https://www.brookings.edu/research/the-testing
-ground-chinas-rising-influence-in-southeast-asia-and-regional-responses.

36. See, e.g., Manuel Mogato et al., "ASEAN Deadlocked on South China Sea,
Cambodia Blocks Statement," Reuters, July 25, 2016, https://www.reuters
.com/article/us-southchinasea-ruling-asean/asean-deadlocked-on-south
-china-sea-cambodia-blocks-statement-idUSKCN1050F6.

37. Brookings Institution, "Interview on China's Belt and Road: The New Geo-
politics of Global Infrastructure Development" (Washington, D.C.: Brookings Institution, April 2019), https://www.brookings.edu/wp-content/uploads
/2019/04/FP_20190419_bri_interview.pdf.

38. Dan Blumenthal and Derek Scissors, "China's Great Stagnation," *National
Interest*, October 17, 2016, https://nationalinterest.org/feature/chinas-great
-stagnation-18073.

39. Henry Kissinger, *Does America Need a Foreign Policy?* (New York: Simon &
Schuster, 2001), 135.

THREE
Competitive Interdependence

1. Henry Kissinger, *On China* (New York: Penguin Books, 2012), 276.
2. Jeff Bader, "Changing China Policy: Are We in Search of Enemies?" (Washington, D.C.: Brookings Institution, June 2015), https://www.brookings.edu
/wp-content/uploads/2016/06/Changing-China-policy-Are-we-in-search
-of-enemies.pdf.
3. Laura Silver, Kat Devlin, and Christine Huang, "U.S. Views of China Turn
Sharply Negative amid Trade Tensions" (Washington, D.C.: Pew Research
Center, August 13, 2019), https://www.pewresearch.org/global/2019/08/13
/u-s-views-of-china-turn-sharply-negative-amid-trade-tensions.
4. Ryan Hass, "A Crisis Is a Terrible Thing to Waste" (Washington, D.C.:
Brookings Institution, January 16, 2019), https://www.brookings.edu/research
/a-crisis-is-a-terrible-thing-to-waste.
5. Dina Smeltz et al., "Rejecting Retreat" (Chicago: Chicago Council on Global

Affairs, September 6, 2019), https://www.thechicagocouncil.org/publication
/rejecting-retreat.

6. Pew Research Center, "Climate Change and Russia Are Partisan Flashpoints
in Public's Views of Global Threats" (Washington, D.C.: Pew Research Center,
July 30, 2019), https://www.people-press.org/2019/07/30/climate-change
-and-russia-are-partisan-flashpoints-in-publics-views-of-global-threats.

7. "Smart Competition: Adapting U.S. Strategy toward China at 40 Years:
Hearing before the Committee on Foreign Affairs," 116th Cong. (2019) (testimony of Elizabeth Economy and Aaron Friedberg). See also Orville Schell
and Larry Diamond, eds., "Chinese Influence and American Interests: Promoting Constructive Vigilance" (Stanford, Calif.: Hoover Institution Press,
2018), https://www.hoover.org/sites/default/files/research/docs/chinese
influence_americaninterests_fullreport_web.pdf; John Pomfret, "Why the
United States Doesn't Need to Return to a Gentler China Policy," *Washington Post*, July 9, 2019, https://www.washingtonpost.com/opinions/2019/07/09
/why-united-states-doesnt-need-return-gentler-china-policy.

8. Henry Farrell and Abraham L. Newman, "Weaponized Interdependence:
How Global Economic Networks Shape State Coercion," *International Security* 44, no. 1 (2019): 42–79.

9. David Shambaugh, "Dealing with China: Tough Engagement and Managed
Competition," *Asia Policy*, no. 23 (2017): 4–12. See also Robert Blackwill,
"Implementing Grand Strategy toward China" (New York: Council on Foreign Relations, January 2020), https://www.cfr.org/report/implementing
-grand-strategy-toward-china.

10. See, e.g., "Remarks by National Security Advisor Ambassador John R. Bolton
on the Trump Administration's New Africa Strategy," Washington, D.C., December 13, 2018, https://www.whitehouse.gov/briefings-statements/remarks
-national-security-advisor-ambassador-john-r-bolton-trump-administra
tions-new-africa-strategy; and Michael R. Pompeo, "The China Challenge,"
speech, New York City, October 30, 2019, https://py.usembassy.gov/speech
-of-secretary-of-state-michael-r-pompeo-the-china-challenge.

11. See, e.g., Laura Silver, Kat Devlin, and Christine Huang, "People around the
Globe Are Divided in Their Opinions of China" (Washington, D.C.: Pew
Research Center, September 30, 2019), https://www.pewresearch.org/fact
-tank/2019/09/30/people-around-the-globe-are-divided-in-their-opinions
-of-china.

12. European Commission, "E.U.-China: A Strategic Outlook," European
Commission and HR/VP contribution to the European Council, March 12,
2019, https://ec.europa.eu/commission/sites/beta-political/files/communica
tion-eu-china-a-strategic-outlook.pdf.

13. John Mearsheimer and Stephen Walt, "The Case for Offshore Balancing:
A Superior US Grand Strategy," *Foreign Affairs*, July-August 2016, https://

www.foreignaffairs.com/articles/united-states/2016-06-13/case-offshore
-balancing.

14. For a fuller description of these schools of thought, see chapter 6 in Thomas Wright, *All Measures Short of War: The Contest for the 21st Century and the Future of American Power* (New Haven, Conn.: Yale University Press, 2018).

15. Hugh White, Mary Kay Magistand, and Zha Daojiong, "It Is Time for America to Consider Accommodation with China," *Foreign Policy*, June 8, 2015, https://foreignpolicy.com/2015/06/08/china-us-policy-rivalry-tension -great-powers-accommodation.

16. Bill Burns, "Assessing the Role of the United States in the World," testimony before Senate Foreign Relations Committee, February 27, 2019, https:// carnegieendowment.org/2019/02/27/assessing-role-of-united-states-in -world-pub-78465.

17. Kurt M. Campbell and Jake Sullivan, "Competition without Catastrophe: How America Can Both Challenge and Coexist with China," *Foreign Affairs*, September–October 2019, https://www.foreignaffairs.com/articles/china /competition-with-china-without-catastrophe.

18. Paul Heer, *Mr. X and the Pacific: George F. Kennan and American Policy in East Asia* (Ithaca, N.Y.: Cornell University Press, 2018), 235.

19. Farewell address by Ambassador Jon Huntsman, April 6, 2011, Shanghai, China.

20. Richard Armitage and Joseph Nye, *The U.S.-Japan Alliance: Getting Asia Right through 2020* (Washington, D.C.: Center for Strategic and International Studies, February 2007), https://csis-prod.s3.amazonaws.com/s3fs-public /legacy_files/files/media/csis/pubs/070216_asia2020.pdf.

21. Ely Ratner et al., "Rising to the China Challenge: Renewing American Competitiveness in the Indo-Pacific" (Washington, D.C.: Center for a New American Security, January 28, 2020), https://www.cnas.org/publications /reports/rising-to-the-china-challenge.

22. Jeffrey Bader, "U.S.-China Relations: Is It Time to End the Engagement?" (Washington, D.C.: Brookings Institution, September 2018), 2, https://www .brookings.edu/wp-content/uploads/2018/09/FP_20180925_us_china _relations.pdf.

23. See, e.g., Lee Hsien Loong, "Keynote Speech at the 18th Asia Security Summit," speech at the Shangri-La Dialogue, Singapore, May 31, 2019, https:// www.iiss.org/events/shangri-la-dialogue/shangri-la-dialogue-2019; Scott Morrison, "Where We Live," speech, Sydney, June 26, 2019, https://www.pm.gov .au/media/where-we-live-asialink-bloomberg-address; Jokowi Widodo, "Indonesia Invites China to Join Indo-Pacific Cooperation," comments at the ASEAN-China Summit, Singapore, November 14, 2018, https://setkab.go .id/en/indonesia-invites-china-to-join-indo-pacific-cooperation; Chan Heng Chee, "Resisting the Polarising Pull of US-China Rivalry," *Straits Times*,

June 18, 2019, https://www.straitstimes.com/opinion/resisting-the-polarising
-pull-of-us-china-rivalry.

24. Ryan Hass, "Principles for Managing U.S.-China Competition" (Washington, D.C.: Brookings Institution, August 2018), https://www.brookings.edu
/wp-content/uploads/2018/08/FP_20180817_managing_competition.pdf.

25. Hass, "Principles for Managing U.S.-China Competition."

26. Hass, "Principles for Managing U.S.-China Competition."

27. Hass, "A Crisis Is a Terrible Thing to Waste."

28. Ryan Hass, "Lessons for Raising Human Rights Issues with Beijing" (Washington, D.C.: Brookings Institution, May 29, 2019), https://www.brookings
.edu/blog/order-from-chaos/2019/05/29/lessons-for-raising-human-rights
-issues-with-beijing.

29. Evan Osnos, "The Future of America's Contest with China," *New Yorker*, January 13, 2020, https://www.newyorker.com/magazine/2020/01/13/the-future
-of-americas-contest-with-china.

30. X [George Kennan], "The Sources of Soviet Conduct," *Foreign Affairs*, July
1947, https://www.foreignaffairs.com/articles/russian-federation/1947-07-01
/sources-soviet-conduct.

31. George Kennan, "George Kennan's 'Long Telegram,'" February 22, 1946,
History and Public Policy Program Digital Archive, National Archives and
Records Administration, Department of State Records (Record Group 59),
Central Decimal File, 1945–1949, 861.00/2-2246; reprinted in U.S. Department of State, ed., *Foreign Relations of the United States, 1946*, vol. 6, *Eastern
Europe; The Soviet Union* (Washington, D.C.: United States Government
Printing Office, 1969), 696–709, http://digitalarchive.wilsoncenter.org/document/116178.pdf.

FOUR

Technology Competition

1. Brad Smith and Carol Ann Browne, *Tools and Weapons* (New York: Penguin,
2019), 267.

2. According to data compiled by LIS, a group that maintains the Luxembourg
Income Study Database, "From 2000 to 2014, the median income in Canada
and Great Britain grew by nearly 20 percent, with Ireland and the Netherlands not far behind. In the United States, median incomes were up just 0.3
percent." A similar story applies to income inequality. "Since the 1980s, income inequality in the United States has risen faster than in any other major
advanced economy, and the level of inequality today is higher than in any
other country in the OECD except Chile, Mexico, and Turkey." See Ted
Alden, *Failure to Adjust: How Americans Got Left Behind in the Global Economy*
(Lanham, Md.: Rowman & Littlefield, 2017), 7.

3.   "Section 301 Report into China's Acts, Policies, and Practices Related to Technology Transfer, Intellectual Property, and Innovation" (Washington, D.C.: Office of the United States Trade Representative, March 22, 2018), https://ustr.gov/about-us/policy-offices/press-office/press-releases/2018/march/section-301-report-chinas-acts.

4.   Alden, *Failure to Adjust*, 161.

5.   Tom Connor, "Trade Wars, Climate Change Plunge the Family Farm into Crisis. Is It an Endangered American Institution?" CNBC, November 2, 2019, https://www.cnbc.com/2019/11/02/trade-wars-climate-change-plunge-the-family-farm-into-crisis.html. See also Chuck Jones, "Amid Trump Tariffs, Farm Bankruptcies and Suicides Rise," *Forbes*, August 30, 2019, https://www.forbes.com/sites/chuckjones/2019/08/30/amid-trump-tariffs-farm-bankruptcies-and-suicides-rise/#766230732bc8.

6.   PBS Frontline, "Trump's Trade War," directed and written by Rick Young, WGBH, May 7, 2019, https://www.pbs.org/wgbh/frontline/film/trumps-trade-war/transcript.

7.   See Robert Spaulding, *Stealth War: How China Took Over While America's Elite Slept* (New York: Portfolio, 2019).

8.   Charles Boustany and Aaron L. Friedberg, "Partial Disengagement: A New U.S. Strategy for Economic Competition with China" (Washington, D.C.: National Bureau of Asian Research, November 2019), https://www.nbr.org/publication/partial-disengagement-a-new-u-s-strategy-for-economic-competition-with-china.

9.   Marco Rubio, "Investing in China Is Not a Good Deal," *New York Times*, January 17, 2020, https://www.nytimes.com/2020/01/17/opinion/sunday/Marco-Rubio-China-trade-deal.html; Michael Martina, "Senator Warren, in Beijing, Says U.S. Is Waking Up to Chinese Abuses," Reuters, April 1, 2018, https://www.reuters.com/article/us-usa-china-warren/senator-warren-in-beijing-says-u-s-is-waking-up-to-chinese-abuses-idUSKCN1H80X2.

10. See Marrian Zhou, "Bill Gates: Paranoia on China Is a 'Crazy Approach' to Innovation," *Nikkei Asian Review*, November 8, 2019, https://asia.nikkei.com/Spotlight/Huawei-crackdown/Bill-Gates-Paranoia-on-China-is-a-crazy-approach-to-innovation.

11. Jonathan Hillman, "Pretending All Chinese Companies Are Evil Schemers Will Only Hurt the U.S. Economy," *Washington Post*, November 8, 2019, https://www.washingtonpost.com/outlook/pretending-all-chinese-companies-are-evil-schemers-will-only-hurt-the-us-economy/2019/11/08/bod98798-00dc-11ea-9518-1e76abco88b6_story.html.

12. Fareed Zakaria, "The New China Scare," *Foreign Affairs*, January–February 2020, https://www.foreignaffairs.com/articles/china/2019-12-06/new-china-scare.

13. China has enunciated its national innovation goals in three primary industrial policies designed to raise its international competitiveness: the 2014

Integrated Circuits Promotion Guidelines; the Made in China 2025 plan; and the Next Generation Artificial Intelligence Plan.

14. For a balanced analysis of civil-military fusion, see Lorand Laskai, "Civil-Military Fusion: The Missing Link between China's Technological and Military Rise" (New York: Council on Foreign Relations, January 29, 2018), https://www.cfr.org/blog/civil-military-fusion-missing-link-between-chinas -technological-and-military-rise.

15. Smith and Browne, *Tools and Weapons*, 253.

16. Robert Manning et al., "The Global Innovation Sweepstakes" (Washington, D.C.: Atlantic Council, June 2018), https://www.atlanticcouncil.org/wp -content/uploads/2018/06/The-Global-Innovation-Sweepstakes.pdf.

17. David Dollar, Yiping Huang, and Yang Yao, eds., *China 2049: Economic Challenges of a Rising Global Power* (Washington, D.C.: Brookings Press, 2020).

18. Dollar, Huang, and Yao, *China 2049*.

19. "Promoting Innovation and Market Competition Are Key to China's Future Growth" (Beijing, China: World Bank, September 17, 2019), https://www .worldbank.org/en/news/press-release/2019/09/17/promoting-innovation -and-market-competition-are-key-to-chinas-future-growth.

20. See, e.g., Barry Naughton, "The Current Wave of State Enterprise Reform in China: A Preliminary Appraisal," *Asian Economic Policy Review* 12, no. 2 (July 2017): 282–298.

21. Scott Kennedy, "China's Risky Drive into New-Energy Vehicles" (Washington, D.C.: Center for Strategic and International Studies, November 2018), https://csis-prod.s3.amazonaws.com/s3fs-public/publication/181127_Kennedy _NEV_WEB_v3.pdf?wJboZdPX5rhUfie1yaPEnws2uKUQJccQ.

22. "The World in 2050," PricewaterhouseCoopers, February 2017, https:// www.pwc.com/gx/en/issues/economy/the-world-in-2050.html; see also OECD, "Real GDP Forecast (Indicator)," 2019, https://data.oecd.org/gdp/real-gdp -forecast.htm.

23. Homi Kharas, "The Unprecedented Expansion of the Global Middle Class: An Update" (Washington, D.C.: Brookings Institution, February 2017), https://www.brookings.edu/wp-content/uploads/2017/02/global _20170228_global-middle-class.pdf.

24. Linda Qiu, "Fact Checking Trump's Claims about China's 'Worst Year,'" *New York Times*, September 4, 2019, https://www.nytimes.com/2019/09/04/us /politics/fact-checking-trump-china.html.

25. Robert Zoellick, "Can America and China Be Stakeholders?" address to U.S.-China Business Council Gala 2019, Washington, D.C., December 4, 2019, https://www.uschina.org/sites/default/files/ambassador_robert_zoellicks _remarks_to_the_uscbc_gala_2019.pdf.

26. Adam Segal, *Innovation and National Security: Keeping Our Edge* (New York: Council on Foreign Relations Press, 2019), 19.

27. L. Rafael Reif, "China's Challenge Is America's Opportunity," *New York*

Times, August 8, 2018, https://www.nytimes.com/2018/08/08/opinion/china
-technology-trade-united-states.html.

28. See, e.g., Daron Acemoglu et al., "Import Competition and the Great U.S.
Employment Sag of the 2000s," *Journal of Labor Economics* 34, no. 1 (January
2016), https://economics.mit.edu/files/11560.

29. Kishore Mahbubani, *Has the West Lost It?* (New York: Penguin, 2018), 86.

30. Segal, *Innovation and National Security*, 7.

31. Alden, *Failure to Adjust*, 151.

32. Alden, *Failure to Adjust*, 144.

33. James Lewis, "Emerging Technologies and Managing the Risk of Technology Transfer to China" (Washington, D.C.: Center for Strategic and International Studies, September 4, 2019), https://www.csis.org/analysis/emerging
-technologies-and-managing-risk-tech-transfer-china.

34. Ian Bremmer, "The End of the American International Order: What Comes
Next?" *Time*, November 18, 2019, https://time.com/5730849/end-american
-order-what-next.

35. Peter Beinart, "China Isn't Cheating on Trade," *The Atlantic*, April 21, 2019,
https://www.theatlantic.com/ideas/archive/2019/04/us-trade-hawks-exag
gerate-chinas-threat/587536.

36. Steven Pearlstein, "Our Current Economic Boom Is a Mirage, and Our Politics Are Going to Break It," *Washington Post*, January 24, 2020, https://www
.washingtonpost.com/business/economy/the-us-economy-is-booming-our
-broken-politics-are-going-to-wreck-it/2020/01/23/21c812ac-3d24-11ea
-8872-5df698785a4e_story.html.

FIVE
Mitigating Risks of Conflict

1. Zhengyu Wu, "The Crowe Memorandum, the Rebalance to Asia, and Sino-
US Relations," *Journal of Strategic Studies* 39, no. 3 (February 2016): 389–
416.

2. Michael O'Hanlon and James Steinberg, *A Glass Half Full?* (Washington,
D.C.: Brookings Institution Press, 2017), 33.

3. Henry Kissinger, *On China* (New York: Penguin Books, 2012), 520.

4. Kissinger, *On China*, 520.

5. G. John Ikenberry, "The Rise of China and the Future of the West," *Foreign
Affairs*, January 1, 2008, https://www.foreignaffairs.com/articles/asia/2008
-01-01/rise-china-and-future-west.

6. As the China expert Taylor Fravel has shown in *Strong Borders, Secure Nation*,
China has been involved in twenty-three territorial disputes since the found-
ing of the People's Republic of China. It has resolved disputes with North
Korea, Russia, Mongolia, Kazakhstan, Kyrgyzstan, Tajikistan, Afghanistan,

Pakistan, Nepal, Myanmar, Vietnam, and Laos. China has not been involved in armed conflict with any of these neighbors since settling the disputes. At present, China maintains six disputes over territory: Taiwan, the border with India, the border with Bhutan, and three island groups. Taylor Fravel, *Strong Borders, Secure Nation: Cooperation and Conflict in China's Territorial Disputes,* Princeton Studies in International History and Politics (Princeton, N.J.: Princeton University Press, 2008).

7. Ely Ratner, "Course Correction: How to Stop China's Maritime Advance," *Foreign Affairs,* June 13, 2017, https://www.foreignaffairs.com/articles/2017 -06-13/course-correction.

8. Michael McDevitt, *The South China Sea: Assessing U.S. Policy and Options for the Future* (Arlington, Va.: CAN Corporation, 2014).

9. Michael Green et al., *Countering Coercion in Maritime Asia* (Washington, D.C.: Center for Strategic and International Studies, 2017).

10. As but one example of the losses that would be incurred through U.S.-China conflict, the RAND Corporation has estimated that conflict would shave from 5 to 10 percent of gross domestic product off the American economy, and up to 25 to 35 percent off the Chinese economy. For further information, see David Gompert, Astrid Stuth Cevallos, and Cristina Garafola, *War with China: Thinking Through the Unthinkable* (Santa Monica, Calif.: RAND Corporation, 2016), https://www.rand.org/pubs/research_reports/RR1140 .html.

11. Private conversation with senior Chinese foreign affairs official, Beijing, China, July 25, 2016.

12. For further information on each claimant's reclamation activities in the South China Sea, see "Asia Maritime Transparency Initiative," Center for Security and International Studies, https://amti.csis.org.

13. Orville Schell and Susan L. Shirk, eds., "U.S. Policy toward China: Recommendations for a New Administration" (New York: Asia Society, February 2017), 23, https://asiasociety.org/center-us-china-relations/us-policy-toward -china-recommendations-new-administration.

14. R. Jeffrey Smith, "Hypersonic Missiles Are Unstoppable. And They're Starting a New Global Arms Race," *New York Times,* June 19, 2019, https://www .nytimes.com/2019/06/19/magazine/hypersonic-missiles.html.

15. Michael Griffin, testimony at House Armed Services Committee Subcommittee on Intelligence and Emerging Threats and Capabilities hearing, March 28, 2019, https://armedservices.house.gov/hearings?ID=AF77B937-326B-4F05 -B613-1A79ED29651C.

16. Frank A. Rose, "Bringing China into the Fold on Arms Control and Strategic Stability Issues" (Washington, D.C.: Brookings Institution, September 25, 2019), https://www.brookings.edu/blog/order-from-chaos/2019/09/25 /bringing-china-into-the-fold-on-arms-control-and-strategic-stability-issues.

17. Rose, "Bringing China into the Fold."

18. See, e.g., "Third U.S.-China High-Level Joint Dialogue on Cybercrime and Related Issues: Joint Summary of Outcomes," Department of Justice, December 8, 2016, https://www.justice.gov/opa/pr/third-us-china-high-level -joint-dialogue-cybercrime-and-related-issues; "Yang Jiechi Holds Working Meeting with US Side," Consulate-General of the People's Republic of China in Johannesburg, November 2, 2016, https://www.fmprc.gov.cn/ce /cgjb/eng/xwdt/zgyw/t1412858.htm.

19. Elbridge Colby, "How to Win America's Next War," *Foreign Policy*, May 5, 2019, https://foreignpolicy.com/2019/05/05/how-to-win-americas-next-war -china-russia-military-infrastructure.

20. See, e.g., Kissinger, *On China*, 542; Michael O'Hanlon, *The Senkaku Paradox* (Washington, D.C.: Brookings Institution Press, 2019).

21. Christian Brose, "The New Revolution in Military Affairs," *Foreign Affairs*, May–June 2019, https://www.foreignaffairs.com/articles/2019-04-16/new -revolution-military-affairs.

22. O'Hanlon, *The Senkaku Paradox*, 5.

23. Colby, "How to Win America's Next War."

SIX
Navigating Great Power Relations

1. Editorial Board, "Foreign Policy in 1964," *New York Times*, March 1, 1964, https://timesmachine.nytimes.com/timesmachine/1964/03/01/issue.html.

2. See, e.g., Ian Bremmer, *Every Nation for Itself: Winners and Losers in a G-Zero World* (New York: Portfolio, May 2012).

3. See, e.g., Robert Kagan, *The Jungle Grows Back: America and Our Imperiled World* (New York: Knopf, 2018).

4. Joseph W. Sullivan, "Every American Should Hope Trump Prevails against China," *The Atlantic*, August 20, 2019, https://www.theatlantic.com/ideas /archive/2019/08/china-vs-democracy/596248.

5. James Mattis, "Summary of the 2018 National Defense Strategy of the United States" (Washington, D.C.: Department of Defense, 2018), https:// dod.defense.gov/Portals/1/Documents/pubs/2018-National-Defense -Strategy-Summary.pdf.

6. Paul Sondrol, "Totalitarian and Authoritarian Dictators: A Comparison of Fidel Castro and Alfredo Stroessner," *Journal of Latin American Studies* 23, no. 3 (October 1991): 599–620.

7. Homi Kharas and Kristofer Hamel, "A Global Tipping Point: Half the World Is Now Middle Class or Wealthier" (Washington, D.C.: Brookings Institution, September 27, 2018), https://www.brookings.edu/blog/future -development/2018/09/27/a-global-tipping-point-half-the-world-is-now -middle-class-or-wealthier.

8. Michael O'Hanlon, *The Senkaku Paradox* (Washington, D.C.: Brookings Institution Press, 2019), 2.

9. For a fuller discussion of the global state of democracy, see the report "Democracy and Disorder" (Washington, D.C.: Brookings Institution, 2019), https://www.brookings.edu/product/democracy-and-disorder.

10. Bruce Jones, "China and the Return of Great Power Strategic Competition" (Washington, D.C.: Brookings Institution, February 2020), https://www.brookings.edu/wp-content/uploads/2020/02/FP_202002_china_power_competition_jones.pdf.

11. Yan Xuetong, "How China Can Defeat America," *New York Times*, November 20, 2011, https://www.nytimes.com/2011/11/21/opinion/how-china-can-defeat-america.html.

12. Shivshankar Menon, "China-US Contention Has Opened Up Space for Other Powers, Including India," *The Wire*, December 24, 2018, https://thewire.in/diplomacy/china-us-contention-has-opened-up-space-for-other-powers-including-india.

13. G. John Ikenberry, "The Rise of China and the Future of the West," *Foreign Affairs*, January 1, 2008, https://www.foreignaffairs.com/articles/asia/2008-01-01/rise-china-and-future-west.

14. See, e.g., press and information team of the delegation to ASEAN, "Declaration on the Award Rendered in the Arbitration between the Philippines and China," European Commission, July 15, 2016, https://eeas.europa.eu/delegations/cuba/6873/declaration-on-the-award-rendered-in-the-arbitration-between-the-philippines-and-china_fr; Robin Emmott and Angeliki Koutantou, "Greece Blocks EU Statement on China Human Rights at U.N.," Reuters, June 19, 2017, https://www.reuters.com/article/us-eu-un-rights/greece-blocks-eu-statement-on-china-human-rights-at-u-n-idUSKBN1990FP.

15. Emily Feng, "China and the World: How Beijing Spreads the Message," *Financial Times*, July 12, 2018, https://www.ft.com/content/f5d00a86-3296-11e8-b5bf-23cb17fd1498.

16. "European Commission Reviews Relations with China, Proposes 10 Actions," European Commission, March 11, 2019, https://ec.europa.eu/commission/presscorner/detail/en/IP_19_1605.

17. Ryan Hass and Alex Pascal, "Why European Partners Are Critical to U.S. Strategy in Asia" (Washington, D.C.: Brookings Institution, November 13, 2017), https://www.brookings.edu/blog/order-from-chaos/2017/11/13/why-european-partners-are-critical-to-u-s-strategy-in-asia.

18. See, e.g., Ben Westcott, "US, UK Hold Rare Joint Drills in the South China Sea," CNN, January 17, 2019, https://www.cnn.com/2019/01/16/asia/uk-us-south-china-sea-intl/index.html; Wesley Rahn, "South China Sea: France and Britain Join the US to Oppose China," Deutsche Welle, June 27, 2018,

https://www.dw.com/en/south-china-sea-france-and-britain-join-the-us-to
-oppose-china/a-44422935.

19. Jessica Brandt and Torrey Tassig, "Europe's Authoritarian Challenge," *Washington Quarterly* 42, no. 4 (December 2020): 133–153, https://www.tandfonline
.com/doi/full/10.1080/0163660X.2019.1693099.

20. Tanvi Madan, "Managing China: Competitive Engagement, with Indian Characteristics" (Washington, D.C.: Brookings Institution, February 2020), https://www.brookings.edu/research/managing-china-competitive-engagement
-with-indian-characteristics. See also Laura Silver, Kat Devlin, and Christine Huang, "China's Economic Growth Mostly Welcomed in Emerging Markets, but Neighbors Wary of Its Influence" (Washington, D.C.: Pew Research Center, December 5, 2019), https://www.pewresearch.org/global
/2019/12/05/chinas-economic-growth-mostly-welcomed-in-emerging
-markets-but-neighbors-wary-of-its-influence.

21. Robert Blackwill and Ashley Tellis, "The India Dividend," *Foreign Affairs*, August 12, 2019, https://www.foreignaffairs.com/articles/india/2019-08-12
/india-dividend.

22. Blackwill and Tellis, "The India Dividend."

23. See, e.g., Bruce Jones et al., "The Stress Test: Japan in an Era of Great Power Competition" (Washington, D.C.: Brookings Institution, October 2019), https://www.brookings.edu/wp-content/uploads/2019/10/FP_20191021
_japan_competition.pdf.

24. Mireya Solis, "China, Japan, and the Art of Economic Statecraft" (Washington, D.C.: Brookings Institution, February 2020), https://www.brookings
.edu/research/china-japan-and-the-art-of-economic-statecraft.

25. Solis, "China, Japan." Japan has been pursuing a diplomatic campaign to codify its quality infrastructure standards internationally, including seeking endorsement of them at APEC, the OECD, the G7, and the G20. Key principles include open access to infrastructure services, transparency of procurement, debt sustainability, and economic efficiency over the life cycle of the project.

26. Solis, "China, Japan."

27. Tang Siew Mun et al., "The State of Southeast Asia: 2019 Survey Report" (Singapore: ASEAN Studies Center, ISEAS–Yusof Ishak Institute, January 2019), https://www.iseas.edu.sg/images/pdf/TheStateofSEASurveyReport
_2019.pdf.

28. Angela Stent, "Russia and China: Axis of Revisionists?" (Washington, D.C.: Brookings Institution, February 2020), https://www.brookings.edu/research
/russia-and-china-axis-of-revisionists.

29. Stent, "Russia and China."

30. Andrea Kendall-Taylor and David Shullman, "How Russia and China Undermine Democracy," *Foreign Affairs*, October 2, 2018, https://www.foreign

affairs.com/articles/china/2018-10-02/how-russia-and-china-undermine
-democracy.

31. Alexander Gabuev, "Why Russia and China Are Strengthening Security
Ties," *Foreign Affairs*, September 24, 2018, https://www.foreignaffairs.com
/articles/china/2018-09-24/why-russia-and-china-are-strengthening-security
-ties.

32. See, e.g., H. J. Mackinder, "The Geographical Pivot of History," in *Democratic Ideals and Reality* (New York: Norton, 1962).

33. Jones, "China and the Return."

34. J. Stapleton Roy, "Sino-Russian Relations in a Global Context: Implications
for the United States," in *Russia-China Relations: Assessing Common Ground
and Strategic Fault Lines*, by Richard Weitz et al., NBR special report no. 66
(National Bureau of Asian Research, July 10, 2017), 37–49.

35. *New York Times* Editorial Board, "Foreign Policy in 1964."

SEVEN
Moving Forward

1. Richard Hernandez, "The Fall of Employment in the Manufacturing Sector," U.S. Department of Labor, Bureau of Labor Statistics, August 2018,
https://www.bls.gov/opub/mlr/2018/beyond-bls/the-fall-of-employment
-in-the-manufacturing-sector.htm.

2. See, e.g., Elbridge A. Colby and A. Wess Mitchell, "The Age of Great-Power
Competition: How the Trump Administration Refashioned American Strategy," *Foreign Affairs*, January–February 2020, https://www.foreignaffairs.com
/articles/2019-12-10/age-great-power-competition.

3. See, e.g., Michal Kranz, "The Director of the FBI Says the Whole of Chinese Society Is a Threat to the US—and That Americans Must Step Up to
Defend Themselves," *Business Insider*, February 13, 2018, https://www.business
insider.com/china-threat-to-america-fbi-director-warns-2018-2.

4. Dwight D. Eisenhower, "Farewell Address," January 17, 1961, video, https://
www.c-span.org/video/?15026-1/president-dwight-eisenhower-farewell
-address.

5. "U.S. Officials to Visit Britain, Pushing for Huawei 5G Ban," Reuters, January 12, 2020, https://www.reuters.com/article/us-britain-usa-huawei-tech/u-s
-officials-to-visit-britain-pushing-for-huawei-5g-ban-idUSKBN1ZB0L2.

6. "Assessing and Strengthening the Manufacturing and Defense Industrial Base
and Supply Chain Resiliency of the United States" (Washington, D.C.: Department of Defense, September 2018), https://media.defense.gov/2018
/Oct/05/2002048904/-1/-1/1/assessing-and-strengthening-the-manufac
turing-and%20defense-industrial-base-and-supply-chain-resiliency.pdf.

7. China used this pattern, for example, with India at Doklam and with Vietnam in various South China Sea disputes.

8. Richard Fontaine, "Great-Power Competition Is Washington's Top Priority—but Not the Public's: China and Russia Don't Keep Most Americans Awake at Night," *Foreign Affairs*, September 9, 2019.

9. Bill Burns, "Polarized Politics Has Infected American Diplomacy," *The Atlantic*, June 6, 2020, https://www.theatlantic.com/ideas/archive/2020/06/polarized-politics-has-infected-american-diplomacy/612778.

10. Ryan Hass, "U.S.-China Relations: The Search for a New Equilibrium" (Washington, D.C.: Brookings Institution, February 2020), https://www.brookings.edu/research/u-s-china-relations-the-search-for-a-new-equilibrium.

11. For the Gallup poll on trade, see "Trade under Trump" (Washington, D.C.: Gallup, 2019), https://news.gallup.com/reports/267386/trade-under-trump-gallup-briefing.aspx; for the Marist poll on "dreamers," see Partisan Breakdown Data, VI (December 2017), distributed by McClatchy-Marist, http://maristpoll.marist.edu/wp-content/misc/usapolls/us171204_KoC/Marist%20Poll%20National%20Nature%20of%20the%20Sample%20and%20Tables_December%202017.pdf; for the poll on climate change, see Brady Dennis, Steven Mufson, and Scott Clement, "Americans Increasingly See Climate Change as a Crisis, Poll Shows," *Washington Post*, September 13, 2019, https://www.washingtonpost.com/climate-environment/americans-increasingly-see-climate-change-as-a-crisis-poll-shows/2019/09/12/74234db0-cd2a-11e9-87fa-8501a456c003_story.html; for the poll on relations with China, see Craig Kafura, "Public Prefers Cooperation and Engagement with China," Chicago Council, October 9, 2019, https://www.thechicagocouncil.org/publication/public-prefers-cooperation-and-engagement-china.

12. Evan Osnos, "The Folly of Trump's Blame-Beijing Coronavirus Strategy," *New Yorker*, May 10, 2020, https://www.newyorker.com/magazine/2020/05/18/the-folly-of-trumps-blame-beijing-coronavirus-strategy.

13. X [George Kennan], "The Sources of Soviet Conduct," *Foreign Affairs*, July 1947, https://www.foreignaffairs.com/articles/russian-federation/1947-07-01/sources-soviet-conduct.

Index

Page numbers in *italics* refer to tables.

Index

Index

Index